P9-DGY-780

MEDIEVAL ROME

By the same author

Mosaics

The 'Painter's Manual' of Dionysius of Fourna
(Translation and Commentary)

Byzantium

Pietro Cavallini;
a study in the art of late Medieval Rome

Byzantine and Medieval Greece
Churches, castles and art of the mainland and
the Peloponnese

MEDIEVAL ROME

A Portrait of the City and its Life

Paul Hetherington

ST. MARTIN'S PRESS / NEW YORK

First published in the United States in 1994

Library of Congress Cataloging-in-Publication Data

Hetherington, Paul.
Medieval Rome/by Paul Hetherington
ISBN 0-312-12348-5. - ISBN 0-312-12349-3 (pbk).
1. Rome (Italy) - History - 476-1420. I. Title.
DG811.H48 1994
945'.632-dc20   94-25907
                                            CIP

Designed and typeset by The Rubicon Press

Printed and bound in Great Britain

Contents

List of Illustrations

In memory of my parents

Author's Note on Church Dedications

All writers on Rome have had to compromise in some way when giving English equivalents for the dedications of its churches. In this book I have used what in each case seemed to be the form that would be most easily understood, and which was consistent with common English practice. So while, for example, 'St. Peter's' is immediately recognizable as the English form of 'S. Pietro', to render 'Santo Spirito in Sassia' in comparable English would produce a bizarre and unrecognizable dedication; 'Sta. Maria Maggiore' seemed preferable to 'St. Mary Major', but 'St. John Lateran' (easily shortened to 'the Lateran') was preferred to 'S. Giovanni Laterano', and 'S. Paolo' (itself an abbreviation for 'S. Paolo-fuori-le-mura') has kept its Italian form.

I Roma: Urbs Aeturna

'Rome: the eternal city'. It was during the second century AD that the Romans first began to use this phrase. Although their city was less than a thousand years old then, its mythical foundation had taken place in 753 BC, and so it was not old by Mediterranean standards. It must have already seemed to them that their city was indeed possessed of some unexplained powers of survival. Now, almost two millenniums on, the modern age can do no more than confirm the miraculous continuity of its history.

For surely no other city can still present such a long and unbroken past. Athens, the other great centre of the ancient world, displays to the visitor a yawning time-gap of over two thousand years; he sees the masterpieces of the Periclean age looking down from the Acropolis over a city built mainly in the last hundred years. Yet Rome can still show us massive physical remains from every age that has passed over her.

But this very continuity of Rome's past existence can make it difficult to establish when different epochs of her history began and ended. In the second century, she had been at the height of her ancient glory, and represented the one supreme world power. During the succeeding centuries the European world view underwent profound changes, and one of the most radical and long-lasting of these concerned the onset of what was later called the Middle Ages. Such changes do not occur rapidly; no single political or military event can usually be seen to offer itself as a kind of intellectual watershed when something as fluid and intangible as the world view of a civilization is concerned. Yet in the case of Rome, it is possible to speak of one relatively brief period of time when the process of change does seem to have accelerated quite rapidly. The early decades of the fourth century have been recognized as a crucial period initiating the change to what became the medieval period. It was the age of the emperor Constantine, the

1

first of the Roman emperors publicly to accept and encourage the phenomenon of the new religion of Christianity. Since the medieval period is so synonymous with the rise and spread of this religion, which was to become the major unifying cultural force in Europe for centuries to come, it is appropriate to look to the age of Constantine for indications of when this process of change might have begun.

It is perhaps the contrast that Rome displayed during the period of her greatest power and her deteriorating condition in later centuries that has been responsible for the view that any period after the third century can only be seen in terms of decline. Athens has no such valid points of comparison, to suggest an equally gradual decay. It was the great historian Edward Gibbon who conveyed so brilliantly, in his description of an evening passed in Rome, how succeeding centuries can there become compressed into one enduring experience: "It was at Rome, on the 15th October 1764, as I sat musing amid the ruins of the capitol, while the barefooted friars were singing vespers in the temple of Jupiter (now the church of the Soccolants, or Franciscan friars), that the idea of writing the *decline and fall of the city* first started to my mind." With the genuinely poetic insight that gave him his immortality as a historian, Gibbon found these words to express the fascination that he felt for the way that Rome could contain successive layers of civilization on one site, and how their succession could feed his historical vision. It was appropriate that it should be evening, rather than the full light of a Roman morning; the Capitol, which as the heart of the imperial city and its most sacred spot, had housed the sacred geese of ancient legend, was now a ruin, and the temple dedicated to the pagan god Jupiter (Jupiter Capitolinus) was the place of worship for a medieval order of Christian monks and ever since making his first resolve, one order of monks had been succeeded by another.

But Gibbon was pre-eminently a figure of the European Enlightenment; for him, a period so intimately connected with the rise of Christianity had to be synonymous with a certain decline in the values that he admired. Yet because his historian's vision was so powerful, and he could convey it so eloquently, Gibbon's view of medieval Rome as merely a history of decay and decline has

2

obscured much that has survived of the very positive glories of the medieval city. This book will seek to show that although the viewpoint of the Enlightenment has its own validity, medieval Rome can nevertheless still offer to the modern observer much that is impressive, much that is brilliant and much in its achievements that are still significant today. In the struggles of the people, the popes and the emperors, there are innumerable lessons to be learned. While the city knew much ugliness, violence and squalor, it could also dazzle with its pride and its rhetoric.

The location of Rome, over half-way down the Italian peninsula, was a factor that affected its destiny time and again. By the end of the third century its position was entirely inappropriate for the administration of an empire that stretched from England to the Euphrates, and thus it was that Milan became the effective capital. And it was from that city that the famous Edict of 313, giving freedom of worship to Christians, was first promulgated. Rome, however, continued to maintain its importance despite its position.

Another factor, closely allied to the geography of Rome which was to influence the course of the city's history again and again during the Middle Ages, was the large area of stagnant and undrained marshes stretching from within the city walls down to the mouth of the Tiber and along the coast. The malarial fevers that rose from these marshes were notorious; one poet wrote of them:

Squalida torpet humus, corruptis stagna, lacusque
Inficiuntur aquis, pigrisque paludibus atrae
Exhalant nebulae ...

(The sluggish earth reeks, and fetid water lies in the swampy lakes; foul vapours slowly rise from the rotting marshes ...)

The dangers of disease from this source were the terror of many of the enemies of Rome, driving off besieging armies and decimating foreign invaders. The Romans, themselves, must have been to some extent inured to these fevers, and those who did survive them, had an in-built advantage in the long history of the city. Again and again it can be seen that the heat of summer was capable of changing the course of history. Scheming conclaves of cardinals, for example, unable to agree on a papal election, would scatter to the hills as the humid heat of the summer months descended, bringing its pestilent toll. It was said that an English bishop, who was also known to be a skilled physician, was made a cardinal by a French pope Martin IV, so that he would be at hand to protect him from the malarial sickness of their common, foreign, home.

Of far greater importance for the fortunes of the city during the medieval period was the simple overwhelming aura cast by the greatness of Rome's ancient past. Again and again it was to be this, that drew significance back upon the city as the centuries passed. It was also the boundless riches of a city, which had been the wealthiest capital the world had ever known, that was to make it the focus of attention for the barbarian hordes that swept into Southern Europe to fill the vacuum left by the departing legions. The first of these, and probably the most famous, was led by Alaric. At the head of his barbarian tribe of Goths, he besieged Rome in the summer of 410, finally entering it on 24th August. The horrors and bloodshed of the sack of Rome by Alaric and the Goths have become part of legend, and vividly illustrate what fate can store up for even the most apparently inviolable of cities.

Although Alaric had shown that the capital of the world was only as vulnerable as any mortal, the Goths having spent a week indulging in the excesses of pillaging, looting, burning and raping that made them a legend, found that the system that they had destroyed could, in turn, destroy them. The food supplies that had kept the population of Rome fed, finally collapsed; the Gothic hordes were soon starving and forced to leave the city, whereupon they marched on Ravenna, on the East coast of Italy, where the emperors had now moved their seat of government from Milan.

Using the hindsight of later history, it is hard to understand the spirit of Rome during those dark years of the fifth century. It is as if the Romans could not believe that they were now a city of the past, and refused to accept that the world had a new orientation. Not only was the 'New Rome' on the Bosphorus coming of age and expanding its defences and territories, but this was even acknowledged by the emperors in the West; for Ravenna had been chosen as their capital precisely because it was a maritime city that faced the East. For the next three centuries it was to provide something of a mirror, which reflected the glories either of ancient Rome, when for instance Galla Placidia (the sister of the emperor Honorius) embellished it with some magnificent buildings, or of 'New Rome' when, after the re-conquest of the city by Belisarius in 540, the Byzantine emperor Justinian initiated a further period of spectacular and innovative building.

Yet in Rome, less than twenty years after the sack of Alaric, a large and impressive new church was built on the Aventine hill. It still stands with its original dedication to Sta. Sabina, and among the carvings on its famous doors is one of the very earliest representations of the Crucifixion. The creative energy of the Romans is a feature that will never cease to amaze as the history of the city unfolds during the medieval period. This church, which would have been a notable achievement at any period, was followed by an even more impressive structure: the basilica of Sta. Maria Maggiore, on the Esquiline hill. More than any other of the great early basilicas, this one retains to this day much of its original character and decoration. In spite of these signs of energy and hope for the future, it was not long before further troubles were visited upon the city. The Vandals descended on Rome in 455, under their leader Genseric, and the city was sacked again. A further sack and pillage took place in 472 when Ricimer, of the Suevi tribe, who had actually married the daughter of the emperor Anthemius, broke down the city's defences, murdered his father-in-law and for a short period ruled the city. The ultimate humiliation for the Romans came in 476. The youthful emperor who was ruling was, ironically, called Romulus (after one of the twins who, according to legend, were the founders of Rome) and Augustus (the name of the first Roman emperor). He was compelled to abdicate (on a handsome allowance) by Odoacer, the first Barbarian king of Italy, and was thereafter known by the contemptuous diminutive of 'Romulus Augustulus'.

An even greater irony, however, is provided by the presence of Christianity which was to furnish the means and the leadership of the revival of Rome. This must have been seen by many at the time as the final extinction of an empire that had lasted for almost a millennium. Indeed, the year 476 has sometimes been taken as the starting-point of the Middle Ages, signalling as it did the end of the only world order that Western Europe had ever known. As one power was extinguished, another was rising in the city by the Tiber. We have already seen how the energies of the Romans, after the calamitous pillages by the barbarian hordes, had been directed into the building of churches, and it was to be the force of Christian Rome that supplanted the spent powers of the old, pagan order.

This new power had been present in the city since the first century, and had been expanding gradually from the earliest days of Saint Paul's stay there until his execution around the middle of the first century AD. The power of the Church continued to develop through the years, with the adoption of the apostolic tradition and the establishment of Saint Peter as, traditionally, the first bishop of Rome. But the legend of how Leo, as the bishop of Rome from 440 to 461, was to turn back the mighty Attila, at the head of his victorious army of Huns, can be held to be at least based on fact. The confrontation actually took place in northern Italy, not (as legend would have it) at the gates of Rome, and was supported by an apparition in the sky of Saint Peter and Saint Paul; but it would certainly seem that Leo was parleying with Attila on equal terms with the most senior of the Roman senators, Avienus. It is therefore clear that from this date, the Christians in Rome, and their bishop, were a force to be reckoned with.

The irony of the situation was provided, of course, by the fact that there had been periodic persecutions of Christians for over two centuries; their growth had nevertheless been sufficiently rapid and well-founded for them eventually to become the most substantial single force in the city, and was to be the source of the revival of Rome as a world power in the later Middle Ages.

This revival was to be slow and hesitant. Again and again it must have seemed that Rome could not survive. But when her fortunes seemed at their lowest ebb, another personality would emerge to revive them. Just as Leo (the first bishop of Rome to be called Pope, as Leo I, and later Leo the Great) came on to the stage in the mid-5th century, another figure, Theodoric, was to follow at the end of the century, although from very different origins. For Theodoric had been king of the Ostrogoths since 475, and had been commissioned by the Byzantine emperor Zeno to overthrow the usurper Odoacer, who had taken the title of King of Italy. Having done so, he ruled independently from Byzantium as King of Italy, and as self-styled King of the Romans from 493. Although he only spent six months in Rome, Theodoric clearly felt himself under a real obligation to restore the fortunes of the city. He repaired and reinforced many of its defences, rebuilt palaces and other major buildings and restored a number of the magnificent mosaics with which the city had, by then, been endowed. It could well be said that Theodoric's reign of 33 years, though only partially spent in direct involvement with Rome, provided the background of stability in Italy which allowed Rome to re-gather her resources, both physical and moral.

The splendours of Rome under Theodoric must have been very evident, judging by the ecstatic comments of a bishop, Fulgentius of Ruspe, who visited the city early in the sixth century. His friend and biographer Ferrandus reported that Fulgentius exclaimed, 'O brothers, how beautiful must be the heavenly Jerusalem, if earthly Rome can shine with such brilliance!'

But if the end of the fifth century was to see Rome protected by the Ostrogoths, in the sixth century it was the forces of Byzantium, the still relatively *parvenu* capital on the Bosphorus, that was to save her from further spoliation. The name of Belisarius must have been greatly honoured in both Old Rome and New Rome, for it was to be this general, the greatest of Justinian's military leaders, who was to come to the rescue of the Romans when they appealed to the Byzantine emperor. In 536, nine years after Justinian had come to the throne, Belisarius saved Rome from the Goths who had occupied the city. In a series of brilliant campaigns, he had conquered the Vandals in both North Africa and Sicily, and then moved up the peninsular to Rome. There he organized further defences and reinforcements, and the Porta San Sebastiano can still be seen as evidence of his skill as a military engineer.

In 537 the Goths launched a massive counter-attack, and after a savagely fought siege, penetrated as far as the mausoleum of Hadrian (later known as the Castel Sant'Angelo). Totally outnumbered, the Romans under Belisarius were still able to repel them, even using as missiles the heads of some of the giant statues with which the Mausoleum was still ornamented. Yet respite was only temporary. Ten years later, when Belisarius was absent from the city, the Goths returned under Totila, took the Romans by surprise and submitted their city to a further sack. Totila occupied it but was swiftly driven out by Belisarius, who came at once to the city's aid. However, he was later recalled to Constantinople, and in 550 Totila once again occupied Rome.

This violent period in Rome's history, where she became the chief point of contention in the so-called 'Gothic Wars', drew to an end in 552 when another great Byzantine general, Narses, was sent by Justinian to recover the city. In 552 he expelled Totila, and so for the fifth time since 536, the control of the city changed hands.

It is interesting to note that during these dark and disturbed centuries, when the Romans must often have felt that the survival of the city as their home was finally at an end, the leaders who saved the day were, for the most part, foreigners. The Byzantine generals Belisarius and Narses, and the Ostrogoth king Theodoric, all came not just from outside Rome, but from outside Italy. Indeed, but for the rising power of Constantinople, the New Rome built by the Golden Horn, Rome, by the sixth century, could never have remained free and unoccupied. But when the city did produce major leaders from its own ranks, they were men of the church. Just as Leo the Great had been the first pope to represent the city when he talked with Attila in the fifth century, so towards the end of the sixth century another major personality came on to the Roman stage in the form of Pope Gregory I, also later called 'The Great'.

He was a man of profound learning and great political wisdom. Before being made pope in 590, he had built up valuable experience both as prefect of the city, and as a man of the church, whereupon he sold his extensive possessions and became a monk. He was sent by Pope Pelagius II to the imperial court at Constantinople, and on his return to Rome was made abbot of the monastery he had founded earlier. His experience at the Byzantine court convinced him that Rome could not rely indefinitely on support from the East, and so he took it upon himself to secure a peaceful future for the Roman people. The greatest threat was now posed by the Lombard tribes, who were expanding southwards down the peninsular. It was possibly Rome's geographical position that, this time, allowed Gregory an opportunity for negotiation. By 593 he had concluded a separate peace treaty with the Lombards, and then appointed his own governors in a number of provincial Italian cities, so securing for central Italy a period of stable government which it had not seen for centuries. It is important to realize that this was achieved independently of the Byzantine exarch - the title given to the 'governor' residing in Ravenna, who represented the power of the Eastern empire. By taking this action as an independent leader of the Roman people, Gregory became the first native Roman ruler to exercise overall authority for almost three centuries. Yet his authority was vested not in a general's armour, nor in the robes of a senator or even those of the city prefect (which he had at one time been) but in those of the successor to Saint Peter, as the head of the Roman church. His enormous impact on the concept and powers of the papacy will be discussed later, but for the present it is sufficient to realize that in the person of Gregory, there was once again in Rome, a figure of sufficient stature to reassert order and the rule of law in the city and its surrounding lands.

Gregory the Great died in 604, and for most of the seventh century Roman ambitions were to remain focused on the occupants of the throne of Saint Peter. Gregory's influence persisted beyond the grave, and in 607, Boniface III succeeded in obtaining from the Byzantine emperor, Phocas, recognition of Rome's superiority over all the other churches. But relations with Constantinople were to remain uneasy, due to differences of race and dogma emphasized by conflicts of political interest. The emperor Constans II, in an attempt to impose unity on an empire that was divided by religious controversy, issued an edict in 648 which forbade discussion of certain religious issues. When this was read out in the Lateran synod in Rome, Pope Martin I refused to accept its implications. He was eventually captured by the Exarch of Ravenna, taken under arrest to Constantinople, and exiled to the Chersonese; he died in exile in Sebastopol in 655. Once again it is important to realize that for the Byzantine emperor, the person of the pope represented the city, and hence the people, of Rome.

It was to be external events which dominated a great part of Roman history for the next three centuries; Romans were never to be allowed to be masters of their own destiny for very long. For a number of years from 685, all the popes were of Syrian or Greek origin; John V came from Antioch, John VI and John VII from Greece, and Constantinus was a native of Syria. The latter died in 715, but the Eastern influence in Roman affairs was to develop further as, during the eighth century, thousands of Greek monks fled to the West to escape the persecution of the Iconoclast emperors in Byzantium. Most of them settled in Southern Italy, but a number arrived in Rome. There was even a Greek quarter of the city, located near the foot of the Palatine hill. Their church was originally called Santa Maria in Schola Graeca, but it was later changed to Santa Maria in Cosmedin. This Eastern influence was to have considerable impact on the arts in Rome, and was encouraged by Pope Gregory III (731-741), who came from Syria, and Zacharias (741-752), who was another Greek.

But further troubles were in store from another direction. The Lombards had again begun to present a threat from the North. Under their leader Liutprand, they had actually reached the gates of Rome when Pope Gregory II (715-731) came out to address him; his persuasive and peace-making speech must have touched a vein of piety and respect for religion in the warlike king, as Liutprand withdrew his troops, gave back the papal lands that he had occupied, and went to pray at the tomb of Saint Peter, in the Vatican. There he left, on the tomb of the apostle, his sword and dagger, his armour and even his golden crown; there could not have been a clearer acknowledgement of his respect for the unique and divine position of Rome as housing both the remains and the successors of the 'prince of the apostles'.

However, Liutprand had no such inhibitions about the city fortress of Ravenna, the seat of the Byzantine Exarch, and so the focus of all hatred of imperial power. He had little difficulty in capturing the city, and so ending the unbroken period of Byzantine control. It is interesting that the Lombards, a strongly Catholic tribe, had immediately declared themselves against the iconoclast edicts of the Byzantine emperors; however, the exarchate of Ravenna seems to have been sufficiently far from the imperial control in Constantinople for the fervour of the iconoclasts not to have reached there. While in Constantinople all the magnificent mosaics of Justinian and his age would have been destroyed, they remain in Ravenna as a brilliant but silent testimony to what has been lost from the city on the Golden Horn. It is also interesting to note that it was the Venetians, at that date still a very modest maritime power, who came to the rescue of the Exarch, and returned his city to Byzantine rule. Later on, there was even for a short time an uneasy alliance between the Exarch and Liutprand, who still viewed Rome as a prize which they would both like to share, but this threat came to nothing.

But for the Roman people, it was clear that the Lombards were a problem that would not go away. They even bought peace for a time from Liutprand's successor, Aistulfus; each Roman man, woman and child who acknowledged him as their lawful sovereign was rewarded with a piece of gold. Looking for more powerful allies who would make common cause against the war-like and unstable Lombards, the Romans turned to the countries North of the Alps, and in particular to the kingdom of the Franks. Once again, it was a pope who represented the entire Roman people, and in 754, Stephen III made the journey across the Alps to request the aid of their king, Pepin. Stephen entreated the king to come to the aid of Rome at once, because Aistulfus, in defiance of a treaty he had made with Stephen shortly before, was besieging the city. He was successful in his pleading, and Pepin crossed into Italy with an army that quickly subdued the Lombards, who withdrew to the North in some ignominy. In 756 they returned to the attack, in direct contravention of the peace terms that Pepin had imposed, but on the request of Pope Stephen, Pepin returned once more and vanquished Aistulfus even more decisively than before.

The significance of these events for Rome, as for the rest of Europe, was to be profound. For the links that were forged with Pepin were soon after to be enlarged and expanded out of all recognition by his son, Charles, known to history as Charlemagne - the first of the Holy Roman Emperors. The appeal to Charlemagne came from Pope Leo III (795-816). He had suffered greatly from opposition to his rule in Rome on the part of the heirs of his predecessor, Hadrian I, and was, in effect, the victim of the internal power-struggles of the Roman baronial families. During a procession on St. Mark's day, in 799, an attempt on the pope's life was almost successful. After recovering from his wounds, Leo fled north to Charlemagne. He was given an escort to take him back to Rome in safety, and in 800, Charlemagne, himself, came there to investigate the charges brought against Leo.

The stage was now set for an act of profound importance for all later Roman history. It could be said that the papacy had now become too important an institution to survive without access to greater temporal power - that the moral authority exercised by the pope was in need of another form of authority to enforce and protect it. The precise frame of mind of the actors who took part in this drama is still debated, as is the exact balance of compulsion and reluctance, but the fact remains that on Christmas Day 800, at a solemn ceremony in St. Peter's, Rome, the Pope crowned Charlemagne as a new Roman Emperor. The congregation, it is reported, burst out with the shouted acclamation: 'Long life and victory to Charles Augustus, crowned by God, great and peaceful emperor of the Romans.' A new force in the political life of Europe had been born.

In spite of the fundamental importance of this event, and its implications for all later European history, there is still uncertainty about even some of its most basic features. Was it the culmination of a long intrigue, or largely unpremeditated? What precisely were Charlemagne's motives? Just what did anyone understand by the term 'Roman Empire', which he began to use the following year, when everyone knew that 'the Emperor of the Romans' governed the empire from Constantinople? Charlemagne himself was clearly uncertain of his position, and the extent and limits of the new Emperor's powers, which were never at any stage properly defined. In the years to come the Roman people, with their strong local pride, were to resent the usurpation of imperial power by German lords who then might abuse their position. For the rest of the Middle Ages there was to be a triangular power-struggle between the papacy, the emperors and the Roman people. Yet at the time it must have seemed a logical and effective course of action. To Leo it was completely clear what had been achieved, and he commemorated his action in a famous mosaic that he had installed in one of the halls of the Lateran palace - which still remained the papal residence. It depicted Saint Peter bestowing on

Pope Leo the pallium, as symbol of his papal authority, and on Charlemagne a standard, symbolizing his sovereignty in temporal matters.

Charlemagne died in 814, but the astonishing political achievements of his reign were not to last long. No single successor was equal to the task of maintaining the huge empire that Charlemagne had built up over some four decades, and by 855, his heirs had divided it into four parts, with Louis II holding the rule over Italy and Rome.

Still further dangers were now threatening Rome, as in the East the star of Islam had been rising rapidly. By 840 the Moslem raiders had captured Sicily and had a foothold on the Italian mainland with the taking of Bari. In 846 they attacked the suburbs of Rome itself, and desecrated the church and shrine of St. Peter's. This had been built on the Vatican Hill outside the Aurelian walls, and so was an easy prey. Once again, a pope of outstanding qualities was to ascend the throne of St. Peter, and Leo IV (847-855), immediately after his election, set about defending the area of the city laid waste by the Saracens, and the 'Leonine city' (as it came to be called) was encircled by high, fortified walls that can still be seen today. He not only left his mark indelibly on the city of Rome, but also showed himself to be a great naval leader. In 849 Leo took command of a fleet drawn from several maritime towns and inflicted a severe defeat on the Saracens off Ostia. But Leo (later to be canonized) was destined to be the last major statesman to occupy the papal office for a long time. As the tenth century progressed the papacy sank to its lowest levels, and there was no alternative power to impose some order on Rome and the surrounding lands.

And so it was again that from outside the city some form of rescue was to come. In Germany, the dynasty founded by King Otto was developing as a successor to that of Charlemagne, and by 965 he had imposed his own rule, and even a pope of his own choosing, on the Roman people. Otto I, to a considerable extent, re-created the Holy Roman Empire that had first been the brainchild of Charlemagne. He devised a treaty with the Byzantine emperor John Tzimiskes, who even gave to his son, Otto II, a Byzantine princess in marriage. She was Theophano, the daughter of Romanus II, and the marriage took place in 972. Already in 967 Otto II had been crowned as Roman Emperor by Pope John XIII.

This re-imposition of law and a measure of stability was certainly bought at a price. There were several revolts by the Romans against their new German rulers. One of these revolts was led by the city prefect, and his punishment was to be led through the streets of Rome seated backwards on a donkey, before being hung by his hair from the bronze equestrian statue of Marcus Aurelius and later sent into exile. The statue was then situated at the Lateran, as a symbol of the common interests of a compliant pope and forceful emperor.

Up to around the year 1000 the empire maintained some form of equilibrium between the Church, the Roman populace and the power of the old feudal and baronial families of Rome and the surrounding states. Otto III had a genuine vision of Rome as the one place where it might be possible to establish a joint rule, with the church as a theocracy, protected and supported by the temporal power of the emperor, himself now the son of a Byzantine princess. But it was not to be. For the next half-century after the death of Otto III in 1002 at the age of 22, the fortunes of the city were guided by a dominant party to the agreement, rather than by an agreed partnership. When one of the Counts of Tusculum, the representatives of one of the most powerful of the families from the hills of the Campagna outside Rome, became emperor in the person of Henry III (1046--1056), they held such a surplus of power that they could impose their own choice of pope on the church, and so ensure an imbalance of the forces of authority in their favour. What was later to be known as the 'Investiture Contest' or 'Investiture Struggle' was now under way.

This dispute, which was to last for much of the twelfth century, concerned the right of lay rulers - the emperor or any other prince - to invest bishops or abbots with the insignia of their office. As such, it was one of the many unforeseen results flowing from the foundation of the Empire under Charlemagne; clearly, no ecclesiastical power could regard itself as independent in any real sense if its officers were appointed by a secular authority which had different priorities from those of the Church. Involving as it did much of Europe, this controversy was far from being confined to Rome, but the city and the popes were crucially important participants in it. Like many such bitterly-contested disputes it was eventually settled by a series of compromises, but not before much anguish and ill-feeling had been expended all over Europe.

For decade after decade the struggle between the empire and the papacy was to dominate the politics of Rome and much of Europe; the Investiture Controversy was just one part of a largely intractable problem. At times the empire gained the upper hand, at other times it was the church and the papacy. There was, for example, the famous occasion involving one of the great popes of the period, Gregory VII who for many years, as Hildebrand, had been a powerful figure in Roman life. His election to the papal throne in 1073 was not pleasing to the emperor Henry IV, who tried to depose him. But as Gregory had stronger support in Rome itself than any other recent pope, he went further than any other pope and actually excommunicated the emperor. This trial of wills ended with the humiliation of the emperor, as he was forced by his German princes to seek absolution from the pope, and to be received back into communion with the church. The famous confrontation took place in Canossa in January 1077. Gregory left Henry IV standing as a barefooted penitent in the snow, outside the gates of the town, for three days before he would agree to see him and grant him absolution. The absolute moral power of a secure pope had been proved a stronger force than the temporal power of the emperor.

But while the Investiture Contest rumbled on, another movement was gaining momentum in different parts of the Italian peninsular. This was to be one of the most important developments for later Italian history, and it concerned the establishment of independent, democratically organized communes. These communes, or city-states, each with their own government and ruling over the territory surrounding them were later, during the Renaissance, to become ruled by despots, and did not finally disappear until the Unification of Italy in the late nineteenth century. But for the development of medieval Italy the movement was a crucial one, drawing its strength from the powerful vein of confident self-awareness that forms such an evident part of the Italian character.

It would never have been possible for the Roman commune to take the same form as those in other parts of Italy owing to its special status as the home of the popes. There was always going to be the makings of a conflict in this respect, and at times this would take very extreme forms. (It is a measure of the difference of the situation in Rome from anywhere else in Italy that it was only in 1929 that, under the Lateran Treaty, the Vatican was established as an independent sovereign state.)

The communes tended to flourish where there was economic prosperity and the papal curia, with its extensive bureaucracy and crowds of visiting clerics, must have been a constant source of considerable wealth to the citizens of Rome. Yet they were never able to forget that they lived in the city that had once ruled the world; if there was to be an emperor in the West, he was only to rule with their consent. There was a continual power struggle through much of the Middle Ages in Rome located round these three interlocking, but often conflicting, sets of interests.

An instance of the interests of the pope and the Roman people being in conflict occurred in about 1140. The Romans had been at war with the neighbouring town of Tivoli, with whom they were bitter rivals. After a hard-fought war and siege the citizens of Tivoli surrendered, but the pope, Innocent II, after accepting the surrender refused to destroy the town. The Romans, who wanted their rival decimated once and for all, broke into furious revolt against the pope's action. They revived the ancient Senate, installing senators that they had themselves elected, and announced that they were now going to be independent of the pope, whoever he might be, as well as of the great noble families. The violence of this episode is indicated by the fact that, after Innocent II had died in 1143, his second successor, Lucius II, attempted to resolve the matter by force of arms. He led the papal troops in an assault on the Capitol, but died of wounds that he received in the course of the attack.

The differing allegiances of the Romans and the popes were to continue, and anti-papal feeling was still running high when Lucius's successor was elected as Eugenius III. Although a considerable statesman in his own right, and not identified with any of the great Roman baronial families and their gross abuses of naked power, Eugenius could not contain the new-found strength and unity of the Roman people. On two occasions he was forced to leave Rome altogether, due to threats of physical violence. The poorer Romans had found a spokesman for their grievances in the remarkable cleric Arnold of Brescia. He was a naturally gifted orator, and a man of great asceticism and personal holiness. He preached that all the clergy should live in apostolic poverty, without wealth or lands or any secular powers, and so his message had a social as well as a political and religious impact. He was excommunicated by Eugenius in 1148 and later, after the pope had concluded a treaty with the new emperor Frederick Barbarossa, he was executed by Frederick and his ashes thrown into the Tiber. But before he met his end he had become the leader of a powerful section of the Roman populace which for a time had control of the city of Rome.

During the twelfth century yet another thread emerged, to be woven into the complex tapestry of medieval Italian politics, and this was the kingdom that the Normans were building up in the South of Italy. It was not to make any great impact on the life of Rome until later, but from the start the Normans represented another power to whom the pope, when he was in disagreement with the people of Rome, could turn without involving himself with the Germanic emperors.

It was also during this century that the phenomenon of anti-popes became almost commonplace in Roman life. There had always been enmity between the great Roman dynasties such as the Frangipani, the Papareschi, the Savelli or the Conti di Segni; when one of their own candidates failed to be elected, they would often proclaim their protégé as pope in opposition to the one who had been canonically elected. In this way there were a number of antipopes in existence during the century without any valid authority beyond the power of their particular supporters. The presence of purely worldly power in the hands of those without legitimate authority naturally led to situations of complete anarchy in the city. Innocent II, for example, was a member of the Papareschi, and had defeated by his election a member of a rival family called the Pierleoni; these had only been converted from Judaism relatively recently, and so had never had a member of their family occupying the papal throne. When their candidate Anacletus II failed to get elected, they set him up as an antipope, and he theoretically reigned for almost eight years. An even greater outrage was inflicted earlier, on Gelasius II, an old man whose reign only lasted for a year; he was actually captured by the Frangipani, who assaulted him and tied him to the back of a mule. He fled to the monastery of Cluny, in central France, leaving Rome in the hands of the antipope Gregory VIII; he died at Cluny in 1119 (his tomb can still be seen there). His successor was actually elected at Cluny, and returned to Rome as Calixtus II. He was able to recover control over the city, and compelled the antipope to ride three times round the city seated backwards on an ass. Later in the long reign of Alexander III (1159-1181) there were actually four antipopes in succession, who were set up by the German emperor Frederick Barbarossa in opposition to the legitimate pope. Alexander had to flee from Rome more than once when his support dwindled and the followers of the emperor presented a physical danger; his papal authority was used, however, to excommunicate Frederick, who was finally to be defeated by Italian troops at Legnano in 1176. He died later on a crusade, drowned in an icy river.

Anarchy was to continue in Rome for the rest of the twelfth century. Urban III, a Milanese pope, never set foot in Rome and died in Ferrara in 1187 after a reign of just under two years. For all this period no one power among the emperors, the popes or the Roman people and their commune was able to exert sufficient authority for long enough to achieve overall control, and so establish some measure of stability. As crisis succeeded crisis, it must have seemed to many that Rome was ungovernable.

It was, in the end, a pope who was to emerge as one of the great leaders of the Middle Ages. Lotario dei Conti di Segni was elected as Innocent III on 6 January 1198, and under him, Rome and the church, were to find a new unity and identity of purpose. His training had been in theology and canon law, and this stood him in good stead throughout his rule of over eighteen years. He was able to establish a dominance over the emperors from the first year of his office, when he used his position to arbitrate between the rival claimants following the death of Henry VI in 1197. Even at this stage, he had the intellectual and moral authority to enforce a new ruling; this was that although the Roman Emperor was decided by the imperial electors, the pope had the right and the authority 'to examine the person elected', and that as it was he who was the person responsible for the blessing, crowning and investiture of the emperor he therefore had, as of right, an ultimate power of veto. All the popes of the previous hundred years would have loved to have had this power, but it was Innocent III who, by sheer force of personality and intellectual prowess, was able to make practice follow theory in this, the most troubled and intractable period of Roman political life.

In establishing the right of the papacy to play a decisive - and sometimes a pre-eminent rôle in secular matters, Innocent brought a substantial measure of peace to the city of Rome, and even to the more remote parts of Europe. The autocratic King John of England, for example, was obliged to recognize the pope as his feudal overlord when he failed, after much bitterness and great political disturbance, to have his own candidate elected as Archbishop of Canterbury.

The same careful legality of approach that was exercised here, on the international stage, coupled as it was to genuine authority, naturally had a great effect in the city of Rome itself. While total peace never ever reigned there, the presence of an effective and widely-respected power in the papal palace at the Lateran, had a substantial effect. This was nowhere better reflected than in Innocent's attitude to the Senate of Rome.

The senate had existed in some form throughout much of the earlier Middle Ages, although there were periods when it completely disappeared. It had been restored in 1144, and proudly issued a new coinage with the ancient device 'S.P.Q.R.' (*Senatus Populusque Romanus* - The Senate and the Roman People). It was through the senate that taxes were raised, troops assembled for the defence of the city and treaties were enacted. The senate even controlled such details as weights and measures. Whoever wished to control Rome had to control the senate, and Innocent would have been the last person to ignore this.

Yet the constitution of the senate was an extraordinarily fluid and haphazard affair. Senators tended to be appointed by a median rather than elected by a mass vote, but their numbers were very variable, and a term of office was only for one year. Thus, in 1147-8 there were 25 senators, in 1150-1, there were 15, and in 1187-8 no fewer than 56, with four representatives from each of the 14 districts of the city. When Innocent came to power, this number had shrunk to just one senator. Naturally he wanted a compliant individual in this position, and seems to have had no difficulty in finding one. But early in the thirteenth century, a bout of inter-family feuding was ended by a treaty which stipulated that the number of senators should go back to 56. Innocent had to agree to this, although he thought it an unwise and impracticable course. He doubtless saw that while he could control one senator, no-one could control so large a number. In fact, the system collapsed within a year, and by 1205 Innocent was again in a position to get one man appointed as sole senator, in this case by himself as a direct act of political patronage.

Again and again during the thirteenth century the senate was the battleground for the ceaseless tribal warfare of the great Roman families. Although it was always an office of historic importance, it was continually abused and degraded by the various forces fighting for control of the city. The aura of the ancient Roman senate could still cast its spell on its medieval successor. Certainly it was when the identity of purpose, and means to achieve that purpose, existed that Rome reached the heights of its medieval achievements.

Such a moment arrived in 1215. Innocent III assembled a major Church Council, now known as the Fourth Lateran Council, which affirmed the supremacy of the Church over all other powers. This Council is always regarded as the summit of the entire medieval papacy, and its effect on the city of Rome must have been overwhelming. Neither before nor since could the Rome of the popes have seemed so closely to approximate to the Rome of the Caesars.

By one of those accidents of history, the age of Innocent, so rich in the display of the unrivalled power of the church, was also to see the birth of another religious movement. Born of the spirit of religious renewal that pervaded the age, the orders of mendicant friars, particularly the followers of St. Francis and St. Dominic, enjoyed the papal blessing. They began to fill the streets of the cities of Italy, and to be seen on the roads of the countryside, walking 'with neither purse, nor bag, nor shoes', forbidden by their rule to hold any property either in common or individually. Innocent approved the foundation of the Franciscan Order in 1210, and of the Dominican in 1216, and this acknowledgement of the positive virtues of Christian poverty demonstrates again his great breadth of personal and political wisdom.

The stability achieved by Innocent's long and wise pontificate was not to survive for long after his death in 1216. There were several very able popes on the throne of St. Peter during the rest of the thirteenth century, one of whom was outstanding, Gregory IX (reigning from 1227-1241), but their lives, and the lives of the Roman populace, were dominated until the middle of the century by the brilliant, but unstable, personality of one of the most famous of the emperors, Frederick II Hohenstaufen, who was something of a sceptic. Gregory, who was a nephew of Innocent III, was eventually to excommunicate Frederick, for although he had a powerful base of support in Rome itself, he could not subjugate the clever, wilful and ambitious emperor, whose aim was nothing less than to rule all of Italy. When Gregory died at an immense age, he had achieved the independent survival of Rome, but at the expense of involving his office in the struggles of international power politics to a greater extent than had ever been the case before.

The inseparability of Rome from the chief European powers and their political interests is well illustrated by the events after the death of Frederick in 1250. In order to build up strength with which to resist the Hohenstaufen, assistance was requested by Pope Urban IV from a new source - the French house of Anjou. Charles of Anjou was the brother of Louis IX of France (later St. Louis), and was in a number of ways an obvious figure to whom a hard-pressed papacy could turn. The pope not only gave him the crown of Sicily, but had him installed at the Roman Capitol as sole senator. This action instigated the dominance of France in Roman affairs from then on.

The independently-minded Roman people could not tolerate this usurpation of their rights, and expelled both the pope and his senator, turning to the youthful Conradin, the last heir of the Hohenstaufen, for help. Conradin, who had amassed a substantial army, was defeated by Charles at the battle of Tagliacozzo on 23 August 1268. This signalled both the final extinction of the Hohenstaufen threat to Roman independence, and equally the firm establishment of French influence in Roman affairs which was to have even more important repercussions. Two months later the sixteen-year-old Conradin was executed. For the next four decades Rome was to be the battleground of another three-cornered conflict, this time between the papacy, the Angevin power and one or other of the great families of Rome and its neighbouring towns.

Already in 1261 a French pope had been elected as Urban IV, and it was only when popes of the powerful Roman families could get elected that Roman political life was allowed to lose its pro-French orientation. The family of the Orsini supplied one such pope, and he ascended the throne of St. Peter in 1277 as Nicholas III. Just as Charles of Anjou had used his influence to have himself appointed as senator year after year, so now Nicholas could impose his own will to a greater extent than had been possible for a long time, and it was certainly his Roman origins which helped him achieve this. The change in the attitude of the Roman people to the papacy can be seen in the way that they welcomed the popes taking up residence in the city. Urban IV and Clement IV had not even set foot there; and it was from Viterbo and other neighbouring cities that papal business had been conducted in the past. Nicholas felt sufficiently secure by the summer of 1278 to issue the important decree *Constitutio super electione senatoris Urbis*, which prohibited any emperor, king or prince or any close relative of any of them, or any noble, from being a senator or ruler of Rome. It is a remarkable comment on the life of Rome at this time that a pope should have issued a decree on secular matters at all, and is a clear indication of the absence of secular leadership among the Roman people. It is even possible that by this decree Nicholas intended to leave the way open so that he could appoint himself as senator, thereby embodying both religious and political offices in one person. Nicholas III was in fact the first pope to be granted senatorial rights, although they were bestowed on him as a member of the Orsini, not in his capacity as pope. The decree was later used to make Honrius IV a senator for life in 1285, Nicholas IV in 1288 and Boniface VIII in 1297. There could be no clearer expression of the need of the papacy to have control of Rome, if it was to be successful in imposing itself on the wider field of international political life. In the case of Honorius IV, who was a member of the Savelli family, there was a double insurance of control in Rome. The Savelli had a great fortified palace on the Aventine hill, and the pope's brother, Pandulfo, was made deputy senator in case the pope himself could not be available when needed. Both brothers were severely afflicted with gout and rheumatism, the pope needing a mechanical contrivance to enable him to raise the host when celebrating Mass, and the senator having to be carried round the capitol on a chair to enact the government of the city. Yet between them they held Rome in their grip, and could retire to their fortress if the people turned against them.

During this period the Roman people seem to have lacked a major natural leader, with the result that their city again became a scene of national political struggles. Such a figure was to emerge in the next century, but the last years of the thirteenth century must have offered a sad and confused picture to anyone contemplating the lot of the foremost city of the world. The dangers of the concentration of power in one individual became starkly clear during the bizarre affair of the election and papal rule of Celestin V. Nicholas IV had died in April 1292, and for two years there was a vacancy, as the college of cardinals could not agree on a successor. At last, in desperation, the cardinals elected (in his absence) a saintly monk, who lived a semi-hermetic life, high on a mountain above Solmona. It would be hard to imagine anyone less fitted to conduct the affairs of Rome and of the papacy than this simple and unworldly monk. Hopelessly suggestible, any cardinal or courtier could manipulate him, and anarchy reigned both in Rome and in the papal entourage. After five months he abdicated (the first and last pope to do so), and although this in itself gave rise to grave legal arguments, it left the way clear for the last great pope to make Rome his home during the Middle Ages.

Boniface VIII was in the tradition of major dynastic popes who had emerged during the last decades of the century. Utterly worldly in outlook, and a skilled and forceful diplomatist, he immediately set about imposing his rule on Rome in as powerful and unequivocal a way as possible. He early on quarrelled with the Colonna family, who were at least as rich as his own tribe of the Gaetani. The Colonna had two cardinals in the sacred college, and they had suggested that Boniface was not a legitimate pope. Boniface had them arrested, excommunicated, and brought before him with halters round their necks, forcing them to kneel and respect him as the true Vicar of Christ.

Boniface's achievements were great, but a man of such pride and vindictiveness could not expect to survive for very long in the volatile climate of Roman power politics. His inception of the Jubilee in 1300 is sometimes held to mark the zenith of the medieval papacy and of medieval Rome, and it is discussed fully later. Three years after this event, however, he was to meet his end, his downfall remorselessly following successive acts of *hubris*. The final act was reached in 1303, after Boniface had alienated his old allies, the French, by enacting a Bull that proclaimed that 'by reason of the need of salvation, every human creature is in subjection to the pope.' The French king could not tolerate such an extreme expression of total superiority, and conceived the plan of kidnapping Boniface and bringing him by force before a church council which alone might have the authority to condemn his acts. The pope was in his family palace at Anagni, away from the malarial heat of a Roman summer, when his French enemies struck. The plot failed in various ways, but the pope was imprisoned in his palace for three days before being rescued by the townspeople of Anagni. The Romans sent an escort to bring Boniface back to safety, but his mind had been unhinged by the experience; he refused all food, beating his head against the walls in a fury of humiliation and mistrust, and died just a month later.

Although the French king, Philippe le Bel, had failed at Anagni to capture the papacy in the person of Boniface, he was to succeed to an infinitely greater degree two years later. In 1305 another French pope was elected as Clement V, and it was under his reign that Rome was to cease being the home of the papacy. Clement had been elected in Perugia, and although made sole senator of Rome, he never entered the city but went instead for his coronation to Lyon. Thereafter for seventy years the papacy was

Sta. Costanza: section of mosaic with portrait head. (Pl. 1)

Sta. Maria Maggiore: detail of mosaic on the triumphal arch. (Pl. 2)

Sta. Prassede: vault mosaic in the Chapel of S. Zeno. (Pl. 3)

SS Quattro Coronati; fresco in the Capella di S. Silvestro: the women of Rome lamenting before Constantine. (Pl. 4)

SS Quattro Coronati; fresco in the Capella di S. Silvestro: the baptism of Constantine by Pope Sylvester. (Pl. 5)

Anagni, the Duomo: the large fresco cycle in the crypt, dating from the mid-13th century, contains this battle scene in one of its vaults. (Pl. 6)

St. Peter's: 17th century water-colour of the nave wall and its severely damaged paintings. (Pl. 7)

St. Peter's: 17th century water-colour showing the appearance of the entrance wall with altars and frescos from various periods. (Pl. 8)

St. John Lateran: apse mosaic of 1290 showing Pope Nicholas IV as a donor. (Pl. 9)

Sta. Maria in Trastevere: 12th century mosaic on facade of church - detail: the Madonna and child in the centre. (Pl. 10)

Sta. Maria in Trastevere: 12th century mosaic on facade of church - detail: wise virgins. (Pl. 11)

Sta. Maria Maggiore: apse mosaic of c. 1295. (Pl. 12)

to suffer what has been called the 'Babylonish captivity' of its exile at Avignon. It was not until 1377 that a pope was to live again in the city that housed the tombs of St. Peter and St. Paul.

Gloom descended on a Rome deprived of its pope. No one could have known at the time how long the papal absence would last. It was not until the 1330s that the present Palace of the Popes at Avignon was built. Until then there had been a feeling that the exile was more temporary. The fickleness of the Roman populace is very apparent over this episode. So often scorning the pope when he was among them, when he was absent they were inconsolable. Deprived of the wealth that the Curia brought to the city, Rome must indeed have been a sad city to live in. It still retained its attraction as a centre of pilgrimage and, no doubt, the Avignon popes would have wished to be associated with this aspect of the city. In 1325 Pope John XXII even arranged for a large and expensive mosaic to be installed on the facade of the great basilica of S. Paolo fuori-le-mura, which was one of the main sites visited by pilgrims to the Holy City. But Rome without the popes must have felt a city bereft.

It must have been a deep human craving for a figurehead, or major leader, that lay behind the event of the coronation of the poet Petrarch in 1341. In an age when illiteracy was still prevalent, it is hard to imagine that the majority of the Roman populace would ever have read or understood the Latin verse of this great and original poet - for it was his writing in Latin, rather than his eloquent Italian, which earned him this unique honour. Yet on an April morning, a great crowd accompanied Petrarch to the Capitol, where the senator solemnly crowned him to great acclamation. The poet recited a sonnet glorifying Rome, and then walked in a great and solemn procession to St. Peter's where he laid the crown he had just received on the apostle's tomb. In the dawning age of classical humanism this event demonstrated the undying power of the founder of the papacy to command ultimate recognition.

But if Petrarch fulfilled the need for a symbolic leader, who gave voice to the aspirations of the Roman people, a few years later a real leader was to emerge who was to shake the established order of the city to its foundations. For many years the baronial families of the Colonna, Orsini, Capocci and Gaetani - to name just some

- had made Rome the battleground of their endless feuding wars. The entire situation was ripe for a major demagogue, and he now emerged in the person of Cola di Rienzo. Of humble birth, he suddenly appeared preaching a political creed with intoxicating brilliance. The vision that he held out to the citizens of Rome was that of a city where their feudal overlords were quelled, where the dying strength of the Empire was subdued, and where once again the rest of the world would look to them as heirs to the ancient greatness of the capital of the world. In 1347, on 20 May, he was installed at the capitol by the Roman populace, and took the title of 'Tribune of the People'. He was accorded virtually dictatorial powers, and his rule began with a real sense of vision and purpose with the calling of a council of city-states which had common interests with Rome. But while he achieved a certain measure of order, both in Rome and in central Italy, as time passed it became clear that Cola was deluded by his own fantasies and *folie de grandeur*. On one occasion he stood on the piazza of the Capitol with a naked sword in his hand, and faced to each of the four points of the compass in turn, crying out 'This is mine!' As the vein of madness that ran through his character (and was no doubt part of the cause of some of his brilliant success) became more evident, the Romans tired of him and turned against him. Cola, as a result, had to flee for his life, and hid for two years in a monastery in the Abruzzi. After further wandering adventures, during which he visited the emperor Charles IV in Prague, Cola returned to Rome in 1354. His mission was to bring some measure of order to the Papal States and to the city, but the cruelty and debauchery which marked his later life, prevented him building up any base of power and security in the city. In October of that year a mob caught him at the foot of the capitol, stabbed him to death, and his corpse was hung by the feet for two days. The anarchy that he had promised the Romans to defeat had, in turn, taken his life violently, and his ashes were scattered to the winds.

Perhaps the main achievement of Cola di Rienzo's turbulent life was the final subjection of the great feudal families of Rome and its region; never again would the Colonna, the Orsini or the Gaetani be able to boast that they held the city in their power. The commune of Rome increased in strength and became more confident of its own powers. The absence of the papacy must also have been a factor during this period of more democratic government, allowing a less artificial economy to develop.

In spite of this new mood, there always remained the hope that the popes would one day return to their natural home. This hope was to become a reality in 1367, when a French pope, Urban V, travelled to Rome. The immediate reason for this was the growing instability of the countryside in Provence, due to the effects of the long Anglo-French wars, coupled with the increasing power of the French king, always eager to influence church affairs. But in spite of the great excitement that his arrival caused, with visits from many of the royalty of Europe such as the Queen of Naples and even the Byzantine emperor John V Palaeologus, Urban was never happy at Rome. He was always (and with reason) nervous of the fickle Roman populace, whose expectations of their leaders had so often turned to violent hatred, and as a foreigner he was terrified of the malarial heat of the Roman summer. The papal quarters were in ruinous condition after long neglect, and the civilized pleasures that he had left behind at Avignon were not compensated by his presence in the city of St. Peter. In 1370 he returned to Avignon, and died later that year.

It was to be his successor, another Frenchman, elected shortly afterwards as Gregory XI, who was to make the restoration of the Holy See to Rome the chief mission of his life. Resisting pressures from many sides to remain in Avignon, he finally set out on his historic journey in September 1376. On 17 January 1377 his galley was rowed up the Tiber and he disembarked at S. Paolo fuori-le-mura. A huge and joyful procession, with dancers, singers, and musicians accompanied Gregory and a crowd of ecclesiastical dignitaries into Rome. The papacy had, at long last, come home.

However, the pope was not to enjoy for very long the ecstatic welcome that the Romans had given him. The winter journey from Avignon had been long and beset with bad weather. His health had never been robust, and the physical strain of the journey, followed by the rigours of Roman winter weather, took their toll. Gregory XI died just over two months after his triumphant arrival in the Eternal City.

The historic return of the popes to Rome would seem to be an appropriate signal for the end of the medieval history of the city. No other easily identifiable moment offers itself as a point of obvious change. While the full flowering of the Renaissance was still in the future, Rome, from this moment, would never be the same again. The last French pope was succeeded by a Neapolitan, Urban VI; the election caused the French faction among the cardinals to set up an antipope back in Avignon, so starting the 'Great Western Schism' that was to last for 52 years. Just as Rome had been the scene of the greatest moments of the medieval papacy, so it was also to be the cause of the most devastating and extreme turmoil. But this is another story; only Rome, the city built on its seven hills beside the Tiber, would always remain.

This sketch of the main features of the history of medieval Rome shows how a number of features recur again and again all through this period. We can see how the city of the Middle Ages was continually dominated by the aura and accumulated wealth of ancient Rome; if it had not been for his factor, it is hard to see how it would have become the prey of so many warlike, predatory forces. This pride in their ancient past may have accounted for the passionate and often violent emotions of the Romans themselves - their notorious fickleness can be seen as the result of a divided loyalty, split between their historic and noble past and their emotional attachment of the moment. Both these features of medieval Rome can be found to contribute to another constant cause of strife in the city - the triangular power struggle that was set up in the ninth century between the Holy Roman Emperors, the Popes and the Romans themselves, and which was to provide the battleground for so much later Roman and European history.

This poses an interesting question: Was Rome a more violent place than any other of the medieval cities of Europe? It is certainly hard to find anywhere else that had known such continuous spoliation and internal conflict. No other city had quite the same range of forces all operating as sources of potential strife, or such an array of intractable powers all pulling at the emotions of its people. The passions that were aroused by these tensions were, as we have seen, extreme and unpredictable, and their causes never disappeared; it was only their balance that changed.

If it is accepted that when a people are at play they lay bare their inner corporate psychology most readily, then we need look no further for a possible answer than the Roman Carnival as it developed during the late Middle Ages. As part of these pre-Lenten celebrations two cart-loads of swine, alive, but bound, were hauled to the top of the Monte Testaccio; these carts were then allowed to run down the short, steep slope to be smashed to pieces at the bottom, spilling their load. The Roman populace would then rush wildly forward crying 'Al porco! Al porco!' and dismember the carcases, joyfully bringing back to their families some of the meat from the messy scrimmage. Lent could now begin. With scenes such as this in mind, a good case can surely be made for violence being an endemic quality of Roman life to a greater degree than in any other of the centres of medieval Europe.

The modern visitor who exposes himself to the character of the modern city can still, at times, feel this undercurrent of aggressive emotion. For Rome does not have charm; it is not gentle or sleepy. Its atmosphere has a harsh cutting edge that can shock with its extreme contrasts and deafen with its clamour. The thousand years of its medieval history were just one period of the city's life when these qualities were given open expression, but they existed before, and can still be felt today.

II The Form and Appearance of Medieval Rome

Medieval Rome was a city without a natural centre. As in ancient times, there were no 'rich quarters' or 'poor quarters'; the palaces and mansions of the rich and powerful families were huddled together with the smaller dwellings and shops of the humbler inhabitants. The growth and development of the city's buildings during the whole of the Middle Ages was subject to no consistent law or plan. It was not until the Renaissance that major popes such as Julius II began to impose some element of order on what had, for many centuries, been essentially the product of piecemeal and unplanned building.

This lack of any coherent framework for the way that the city might have developed during the medieval centuries was compounded by the purely historical accident of the location of some of the major Christian sites. The Roman cemetery which was revered as the burial-place of St. Peter was outside the city of Rome altogether on the Vatican Hill, and the grave of St. Paul was several miles to the south, on the Via Ostia. The great basilica that rose on this site was even called 'S.Paolo-fuori-le-mura', or 'St. Paul's-outside-the-walls'. In the same way the shrine of the martyr St. Lawrence, to name just one of the lesser sites that grew up outside the ancient city walls, was on the Via Tiburtina due east from St. Peter's, and again was designated as 'fuori-le-mura'. As the centuries passed, factors such as the growth in the numbers of pilgrims to these shrines, and the continuous services that they needed, coupled with the gradual increase in business at the papal curia and the development of Rome as a centre of international church government, inevitably brought about changes in the way that the population of Rome was housed.

By far the most significant of these changes was already under way in the sixth and seventh centuries, and constituted the biggest shift in population and use of the area enclosed by the city walls that was to occur until modern times. It involved the gradual depopulation of the more eastern areas, near to the Esquiline and east of the Forum and Colosseum, and the corresponding concentration of all activity in the parts of the city against the banks of the Tiber, particularly in the tighter of the bends, and into the 'Leonine City' mentioned in the last chapter. The eastern parts of the city, as they became emptier, and given over largely to farms, vineyards and fields for grain crops, came to be known in the sixteenth century as the Disabitato, while the more thickly populated parts were called the Abitato. This change only took place very gradually. Its main forms had been established well before the eleventh century, but the two centuries after then, until the papal migration to Avignon, saw much consolidation of the 'abitato' as it became to a greater extent the hub of an international organization. It is also from that period that records of building, street names, land boundaries and rents become more numerous, and a more detailed picture can be built up of how Rome, and the housing of its population, developed.

But all the changes that occurred in the shape and appearance of medieval Rome were governed not only by the needs and movement of the population, but also by the overwhelming presence of survivals from the city's ancient past. These were not just the thoroughfares and other open spaces, but also hundreds of built structures, many of them of enormous size. There is no better way to demonstrate the impact that these made on the appearance of the city than to read the most popular of the medieval pilgrims' guides to Rome - the *Mirabilia Urbis Romae*, 'The Wonders of the City of Rome'. In use from the twelfth century, it was written for the benefit of pilgrims and other visitors, and so reflects both the interest in the ancient remains to be seen in Rome, and the relative importance that they held within the other aspects of the city. It has 32 chapters, or sections; the first begins 'The walls of Rome have 361 towers, 49 bastions, 12 gates, and are 22 miles in circumference, not counting Trastevere...' and continues in this vein. The first seven sections list the names of the city gates, the triumphal arches, the seven hills, the baths (ten are named here), the palaces and theatres. Only with the eighth section does the guidebook begin to mention Christian sites, but very soon returns to the secular marvels of the city, listing its bridges, and giving

31

background stories to the few pieces of antique sculpture that were still to be seen, such as the bronze equestrian statue that was then at the Lateran, and the so-called 'Horse-tamers' on the Capitol. The popularity of the *Mirabilia* cannot be disputed; besides appearing in many Latin editions, it was also translated into a number of other languages, and held its own in this field for over two centuries.

As these reminders of ancient Rome were clearly both prominent and famous during the medieval period, some of the foremost among them should be mentioned individually. Pride of place was always given to the Colosseum, that towering mass of masonry that can still send a shudder down the spine of a modern visitor. So much did the Romans identify with it that a Latin verse was repeated often (wrongly ascribed to the English historian St. Bede): 'As long as the colosseum stands, Rome stands; when the colosseum falls, Rome falls; when Rome falls, the world falls.' Great indeed must have been the terror when, during a series of earth tremors that lasted for a month in 1231, part of the Colosseum collapsed, shedding huge fragments of masonry which crashed to the ground.

But while the Colosseum was a unique structure, most of the other classical remains existed in larger quantities. Among the triumphal arches, most of which still exist today, the medieval visitor to Rome would have been shown those of Constantine and Septimius Severus, and he would probably have passed through one as he left the Forum area, known as 'Noah's Arch' - a typical medieval corruption of 'Arch of Nerva'. The two huge columns, each decorated with carved reliefs, and named after the emperors Marcus Aurelius and Trajan who were their originators, would also have been proudly pointed out. Another interesting survival was the presence of several of the ancient Roman aqueducts, some of them still in use, or restored to the point where their use could be resumed. Among these, a visitor could hardly fail to notice the Sabbatina aqueduct, supplying water to the fountain in the atrium of St. Peter's and to the bath, close by, that was used by the multitudes of pilgrims. Pope Hadrian I (772-795) had had this repaired, as well as the 'Aqua Claudia', supplying water copiously to the Lateran area. Ruins of the great Roman baths would also have been very prominent - those of Caracalla and of Trajan, even today, have an awesome sense of scale. Likewise, the ancient theatre buildings of Marcellus and Pompey would have also been a source of medieval wonder, and even a measure of fear. Alcuin, the scholar from York whom Charlemagne brought to his court, wrote these lines in a poem in praise of Charlemagne when he was made the first of the Holy Roman emperors

Roma, caput mundi, mundi decus, aurea Roma,
nunc remanet tantum saeva ruina tibi...

('Rome, the light and capital of the world, golden Rome, there remains to you now only a great mass of cruel ruins.')

The sense of savage desolation that these words evoke, drives home the overwhelmingly powerful impact made by these ever-present reminders of Rome's ancient past.

The Romans were also able to make good use of such buildings as the imperial mausolea erected by the emperors. The most prominent, the mausoleum of Hadrian, would have certainly been seen by every pilgrim to Rome as he crossed the Tiber to go to St. Peter's. From the time of Pope Gregory the Great, who was said to have had a vision in which he saw the Archangel Michael standing on top of it, this was known as the Castel Sant'Angelo. This is a clear reference to its evident usefulness as a fortress, and we saw in the previous chapter how it played a crucial rôle as a bastion of the city's defence during the Gothic Wars; its later history also saw it used for this purpose on several occasions. The mausoleum of Augustus, although smaller, also became a fortress during the Middle Ages.

The fate of the many pagan temples of the city during the medieval period is also of interest. It might have been thought that the obvious use for a place of pagan worship would be to turn it into a place of Christian worship, yet although this did happen in some cases, it was by no means the rule. The public practice of the pagan cults was forbidden by a law passed in 346, and within twenty years all the temples of the city had been closed and their financial supplies cut off. In another decree of 408, it was expressly stated that all temple buildings must be put to a new use, but their automatic Christianization was certainly not stated, nor probably even intended. It was not until 609 that the first such conversion took place, and it was carried out in the case of what was probably the most famous of the city's temples, the huge, domed, circular structure, dedicated to the worship of 'All the Gods', the Pantheon. Only minimal physical changes were made, with the erection of an altar in the main niche; the dedication, which it still retains, was to 'Sta. Maria Rotonda'.

Yet there must always have remained a feeling that Christian worship should not be practised where pagan cults had been celebrated, as direct conversions of this kind were surprisingly rare. In some cases, small oratories or chapels were built inside temples; this was the case in the temple of Minerva, where the Dominicans, later in the thirteenth century, were going to build the large church of Sta. Maria *Sopra Minerva*, or 'above Minerva'. Where Sta. Maria in Aracoeli now stands, there had been a temple of Juno Moneta in which an earlier chapel had been erected, and the huge temple of Jupiter on the Capitol had embedded in its ruins a relatively small chapel which was where the monks were heard by Gibbon singing vespers on that evening in 1764. But these appear to have been the exception rather than the rule. A temple dedicated to Serapis had been converted by the tenth century to a family residence, and another, on the Forum, had begun to be used as a granary. Probably the majority of pagan temples which were not used as quarries for marble had had private houses built inside or against them, or been given some other secular use, by the end of the tenth century. Those that had in some form been adapted to Christian worship by then, retained this use, but were often built over again during the later Middle Ages.

But although the anonymous author of the *Mirabilia* says so little about the Christian monuments of Rome, they must nevertheless have presented an immensely impressive series of experiences to the medieval visitor to the city. The huge, early Christian basilicas such as St. Peter's, S.Paolo-fuori-le-mura and Sta. Maria Maggiore, with their spacious naves and aisles lined by softly glowing columns of antique marble, and the candles and lamps in the sanctuary glinting and reflecting on the mosaics in the apse, would be a memory that he would carry with him for the rest of his life. In the same way, the untold numbers of smaller churches, the monasteries, the convents, the oratories and the chapels, whether adapted from earlier structures or forming part of the architectural history of the city as new designs in their own right, would all have contributed to a unique and overwhelming impression of *Roma felix*. Here are some of these Christian buildings, most or all of which any diligent visitor to the city would have visited.

Pride of place would always have been taken by St. Peter's, followed at once by S. Paolo-fuori-le-mura. These, with St. John Lateran, were the most venerable of the great Christian buildings of Rome, but while the Lateran would always have been included on any pilgrim's itinerary, it did not house anything as sacred as the grave of one of the two greatest of the apostles. All three of these conformed to the type of building known as a basilica. In Rome, this normally took the form of a large, high nave, flanked by two or four lower aisles, and with a series of windows above the level of the aisles lighting the body of the nave. As a building type, it had been in use all over the Roman world for public gatherings, and so was a natural kind of structure to be developed for church use. Usually built with a wooden roof, the largest could hold congregations of two or three thousand, and its use was continued in Rome for several centuries. The three just mentioned all dated from the first age of church building under Constantine, but the fifth century saw such magnificent buildings as Sta. Maria Maggiore, Sta. Sabina, Sta. Pudenziana, S. Pietro in Vincoli and S. Clemente rise to vie with the still towering reminders of the pagan past of Rome. While the variations in the design of these basilicas, often still very evident today after centuries of alteration and restoration, would largely have been lost on a medieval visitor to Rome, he would have still carried away with him a powerful impression of their grandeur and scale. He would also certainly have spent considerable time studying the series of paintings and mosaics which decorated the walls of all the major church buildings, and discussed their subjects with his companions. These 'bibles for the illiterate' were an important and influential source of church teaching and history during the whole medieval period, and some of those in the Roman churches were, because of their siting and authenticity, to be found repeated in abbreviated form in other countries far away.

But besides these larger, impressive buildings, mostly from earlier centuries, there were always hundreds of smaller churches. Some of these would have been built to house relics of martyrs, or the graves of saints, and so might have taken the form of a shrine; it was even possible for buildings with a purpose such as this to be circular in form, enclosing in their centre the particular grave or relic which was the reason for the church having been built.

These structures would have been found dotted all over Rome, with no pattern to their distribution; they would also have been subject to constant change. Some could be renovated or restored, converted to use as convents or monasteries, or back again, as individual patrons or orders came and went. Others could fall into disuse and, in the course of time, collapse, becoming a quarry for building materials which in turn would be used for other buildings. It is this constant ebb and flow of the city's very fabric which conveys so strongly the feeling that Rome was like an organism that perpetually renewed itself.

Equally subject to change, or even more so, was the housing of the inhabitants of Rome. Apart from the gradual large-scale shift towards the Tiber and the establishment of the *disabitato*, the dwellings of both rich and poor would always develop in their own individual way. As families prospered, they would buy up neighbouring land and properties and expand their holdings or businesses. In the later Middle Ages, records of changes in ownership and usage of property begin to reveal quite a vivid picture of the kind of life lived by the humbler levels of the Roman population. Although streets were often very narrow, (even today the major thoroughfares surviving from classical times, such as the via del Corso, are narrow by modern standards) most houses would seem to have had some form of garden, with space for one or two trees and a few rows of vegetables. All poorer housing would have been quite low in height, never more than two storeys, with very modest ground areas. Access was from the network of winding alleys that still can be walked through between the Tiber and the Corso.

Questions of housing lead naturally to the size of the population of medieval Rome. Many guesses have been made on this subject, but with lack of reliable evidence one can only surmise. It certainly fluctuated widely during the thousand years between the fourth and fourteenth centuries, moving from somewhere between half a million and a million in the age of Constantine, down to probably 20,000 or 30,000 at the low points of the city's life when, for example, there was an epidemic of malaria in the city in 1167. It was, of course, for most of its history, a city with a large transient population, and even defining who were inhabitants and who were just long-term visitors (particularly among the numerous clergy) would further confuse the issue. It is probable that if an average for the population between the ninth and thirteenth centuries could ever be established, it would be somewhere between 40,000 and 80,000. Although modest by modern population levels, for a medieval city this was still very large.

Another feature which emerges from the housing records of medieval Rome is how important ownership, and clearly provable ownership, must have been. Not only the private housing of individual families in the narrow streets of the *abitato*, but moving up the scale of status and wealth, the larger mansions and even usable classical ruins had clearly stated owners. It might come as something of a surprise to a modern visitor to learn that a family (in this case the Colonna) were the owner-occupiers of the Mausoleum of Augustus in the later twelfth century, and that the Arch of Constantine was actually owned by an order of monks. All classical buildings that could be used were built on and against, providing as they did a secure base for lean-to structures of all kinds, and each bit of building was carefully recorded for legal ownership. Rights to some classical remains could be quite lucrative; the column of Marcus Aurelius, for example, was owned by the monastery of S. Silvestro in Capite during the tenth century, and a twelfth-century inscription makes it clear that they charged pilgrims a fee for allowing them to climb the column by its internal spiral staircase and view the city from the top. Family fortunes could change rapidly when popes were elected or died, and different clans exchanged influence. This meant that questions of ownership were important, because key buildings would change hands. As the influence of the Frangipani family dwindled, they had to give up ownership of the Colosseum to the more powerful Annibaldi, and, also in the later thirteenth century, the Theatre of Marcellus was bought by the Savelli from the Pierleoni.

Just as Roman medieval history is dominated by the concept of the family - the spreading, amorphous, extended family that protected and promoted its own against all outside threats - so the internal geography of Rome emerges again and again as having its various sectors and areas under the control of one of these families. While this 'dynastic map' of the city would be subject to change at any time, it is still possible to speak of the various areas of the city as being in an almost literal sense the 'property' of a particular family or dynasty. During the thirteenth century the Orsini family grew steadily in power and influence, and spread their holdings of land and property from the area just north of the Tiber island (around the present Piazza Farnese) up towards the Vatican. They finally secured the election of their first pope in 1277, when Giovanni Gaetano Orsini ascended the throne as Nicholas III. He at once speeded up the acquisition of land round St. Peter's, and became the first pope to make his dwelling in a palace at the Vatican rather than at the Lateran. In the same way the Savelli family controlled the hilly stretch of territory running from the Theatre of Marcellus (which they owned) northwards towards the Quirinal. This practice also grew up in the areas immediately outside Rome, with the Gaetani owning all the land round Anagni, and the Colonna ruling the countryside round Palestrina from an ancient Roman palace that they had expanded and fortified.

Control of these areas was very much a physical, even a military, matter. It was achieved above all by the building and use of towers. The author of the *Mirabilia* does not mention them at any point, presumably because they were such a self-evident feature, but on top of most of the great classical monuments of ancient Rome there would have been one or more of these towers to help defend the monuments against all predators. The arch of Titus was so heavily fortified in this way that it was referred to as the "seven-branched candlestick"; its owners, the Frangipani family, had simply made it the base of their family fortress. The same fate had befallen the arch of Severus in the early twelfth century, half of which had been converted into a church, and the other half into a small fortified castle.

These towers would have sprouted up in every part of the city, the *disabitato* as well as the *abitato*, overlooking the main thoroughfares, dominating bridges and all key areas and vantage points. The two most formidable and spectacular were the Tor' de Conti and the Torre delle Milizie. They were truly huge and massive structures, the ownership of which went with a family title. These, with the hundreds of lesser towers must have formed a dominant feature of the city's life and appearance throughout the Middle Ages.

From time to time, when a new and powerful leader came to power, there would be a purge, when some of these towers would be torn down. Sometimes only a few would topple; take the example of the Cenci family who had built a tower in 1074 which effectively controlled all the traffic on the Ponte S. Angelo, the main bridge over the Tiber used by pilgrims visiting St. Peter's. Just the previous year Gregory VII, of the Aldobrandeschi, had been elected pope and apart from the enmity that existed between the two families, he could not tolerate this kind of interference, and so had it demolished.

These towers made such an impact on the general appearance of Rome, due to their sheer numbers, that a twelfth-century visitor to the city wrote that his first impression of it when he saw it from a hill-top was of a 'corn-field of towers'. They were so popular because they provided a natural base from which to launch inter-family skirmishes, and in many cases might be no more than a bow-shot apart. They were such a menace to public order that destruction of them sometimes took place on a large scale. In the 1250s the Roman people had elected as sole senator the Bolognese Brancaleone degli Andalò, specifically as their champion against the all-powerful and turbulent nobility; the towers of these families were both a symbol and a source of their power. Brancaleone, it is said, had no less than 140 of these towers demolished in an effort to reduce their owners to some measure of lawful behaviour.

Although the history of medieval Rome was full of minor family feuds conducted from, in, around and between these towers, only a score or so can still be seen, and these are much altered. The Torre del Papito has been preserved in denuded and sad isolation on the Largo Argentina, and the Torre della Scimmia can be seen from the via della Scrofa, to name just two, but they have been substantially changed. The gigantic base of the Tor de' Conti still stands, and although only the first hundred feet or so are still to be seen (probably less than half its greatest height, reached in the fourteenth century) it takes little imagination to visualize how it would have completely dominated the surrounding area, and particularly the routes from the Vatican to the Lateran, and from the Colosseum to the Capitol. The family who held the Tor de' Conti could have imposed their will on a substantial sector of Roman life.

There is one other kind of tower that should be mentioned, and this is the bell-tower, or campanile, that stood beside many of the churches of Rome. By a happy accident of history, a number of these have survived, and they form a gentle and decorative contrast to the threatening and fortified aspect of the private towers. While the baroque architects of the Counter Reformation have clothed so many of the city's churches with the restlessly curving volutes and pediments of a later style, there are a number of cases where the campanile has been left mercifully alone. Those at Sta. Croce in Gerusalemme, S. Giorgio in Velabro, S. Silvestro or SS. Giovanni e Paolo can all speak today for the many such bell-towers that have not survived from the scores or hundreds that must at one time have existed. Their design was always more open, with the sequence of storeys in which they were built emphasized by arched openings, and with columns of coloured marble or ceramic inserted into the exterior brickwork. Although not exclusive to Rome, these must have still formed a distinct part of the general appearance of the city.

We can now perhaps visualize the first sighting of medieval Rome as it would have appeared to a medieval visitor on first entering it, at some time during the twelfth and thirteenth centuries. The great majority of pilgrims from the north would have entered first not the city of Rome itself, but the Leonine city containing St. Peter's and all its supporting systems for pilgrims. This distinction between the 'two cities' was kept for much of the Middle Ages, but by the thirteenth century would have, to a large extent, disappeared. But we will picture our visitor entering not through the Porta Sancti Petri, but through the Porta Salaria or the Porta Nomentana.

While the roadway might have been quite busy with fellow-travellers, farmers, peasants and other traders bringing their produce for sale in the city, as soon as any visitor had passed through either of the entrance gates - which might have been relatively crowded - and struck off into the vast area enclosed by the walls, he would feel engulfed by the huge and towering silence of the massive ruins which at once came into his vision. His route would have skirted the massive and threatening remains of the Baths of Diocletian (where the poet Petrarch was later to climb up on to the ruinous roof to admire the view); and even today this huge structure has a daunting aura, although completely re-modelled by Michelangelo during the sixteenth century. Our visitor would have seen many houses nestling among the ruins, built up against the secure bulk of the Roman masonry; this would have been where the farmers lived who tended the vineyards and fields both inside and outside the Aurelian walls. One can imagine that any newcomers would have been awed by the scale and menacing grandeur of these remains. The eleventh-century Arch-bishop of Tours, Hildebert, must have had in mind just such an experience when he wrote the lines:

> Par tibi Roma nihil, cum sis prope tota ruina
> Quam magna fueris integra fracta doces.

(Nothing is equal to thee, O Rome, even though thy ruin is almost total; for thy ruins speak more eloquently than thy former great-ness.)

Our visitor would then probably have continued down into the valley of the Quirinal, where he would still be passing through relatively rural parts, with some crops growing, and goats and cattle grazing on the slopes rising on either side. His route would then open out and veer round to the right, as he left the Forum and temple area of Nerva on his left. Moving then into the Forum of Caesar, our visitor would by then have seen both a number of the towers of the minor Roman families, and probably something of the major basilica of Sta. Maria Maggiore on the Esquiline. Smaller churches such as SS. Servio e Bacco and Sta. Maria in Capitolio, on the Capitol, would come into view as the visitor progressed towards the Tiber. He might well pause in the Forum of Trajan, and gaze for a while at the reliefs on the huge column that stood there. A small chapel would have stood beside the column, and if he so wished he could have paid a small fee to the monk he would have found there for the privilege of being allowed to climb the steps inside the column and see the view from the top.

From time to time as he made his way through the ruins round the Roman forums, and past the Capitoline hill, it would be likely that a visitor might see smoke rising from furnaces where marble, stripped from ancient buildings, and even sculpture as it was dug up, was burnt to provide lime from which medieval Roman builders made their mortar. This practice was often lamented by writers on Rome in the later Middle Ages, such as Petrarch, and even continued in the sixteenth century.

As he approached the Tiber the dwellings of the *abitato* would become denser, and he would be able to pause and buy food or other necessities as he walked through the streets now leading northwestwards towards the Ponte S. Angelo. Most of the streets in this area of Rome still follow the same route as they did during the medieval period, when the Tiber bend enclosed the bulk of the city's population. It was also this part of the city that was most affected when the Tiber flooded its banks, inundating whole areas of the *abitato*. This happened time without number, although it would probably have occurred during the winter months when visitors would have been less numerous.

Other distractions on the way towards the Ponte S. Angelo might have included a detour to admire the splendour of Sta. Maria Rotonda (the Pantheon of ancient Rome), stripped by then of its sheets of marble cladding which had covered the exterior walls, but still a source of great pride to all Romans. From there a short walk would have taken the visitor through to the open space of the old Roman Circus of Domitian. There he would have found a typical use of a large Roman ruin, with the vaults and arches of the surrounding seating used as houses or chapels. The area at that time would have taken its name of Sant' Agonale from the oratory to Sant' Agnese which formed one of these chapels among the ruins, and which is still preserved under the baroque church designed by Borromini in the seventeenth century. If our visitor was in the Piazza Agonale at the time of the Roman Carnival, he would have seen preparations for the seasonal celebrations: processions leading flower-decked bulls through the streets, and, in the later Middle Ages, jousting in the Piazza.

When he eventually crossed the bridge into the Leonine City, he would be faced with the magnificent spectacle of the ancient Mausoleum of Hadrian, known throughout the Middle Ages as the Castel S. Angelo. It would still have had its surrounding ramparts, giving it a truly forbidding and military aspect. Its use as a fortress would make it unlikely that its interior could be visited, as it can be today. With the universal goal of a visit to St. Peter's, the traveller would now turn to his left and enter an area called the Borgo.

This was in effect a separate township, developed during the later Middle Ages largely for all the services needed to keep the Vatican area supplied. On the way to the square in front of St. Peter's there would have been many shops, stalls, places for buying hay and fodder for horses, money-changers, and compounds where the various nationalities visiting the city could be lodged. Pilgrims would in this way be housed with fellow-country-men. When he finally reached the area in front of St. Peter's - the Piazza S. Pietro - the visitor who had travelled so far to worship at a shrine so famous and illustrious might well have experienced a slight sense of anticlimax. For the Piazza was not the grandiose and supremely impressive space that Bernini left for the modern world, but a rather untidy and shapeless area, with the steps leading into the atrium of St. Peter's seen across an uneven, open piece of ground, with further houses down one side; a fountain and a wash-house were in evidence and there would have been further clusters of minor buildings and lean-to structures - more stalls, for sellers of religious objects such as pilgrims' badges, candles, holy oil from the lamps at the grave of St. Peter, small icons, and so on, as well as possibly some cells for hermits or the old and infirm visitors. It is important to realize how essentially unplanned and haphazard the development of all building in medieval Rome must have been. But these feelings of disappointment would have been soon forgotten as the pilgrim was absorbed into the excited crowds that pressed into the great basilica, surging through the atrium with its covered colonnades and eventually entering the great doors of the most hallowed building in the Western world.

While the sheer scale of St. Peter's is comparable with the very largest of the medieval cathedrals of Europe, and to that extent might have offered an experience that it was possible to achieve elsewhere, the aura cast by its origins and by the grave that it housed made it totally unique. The gigantic antique columns that lined the nave focused attention on the shrine of St. Peter itself, distinguished by lamps burning as well no doubt as by the throngs for whom this would have been the fulfilment of a lifetime's expectation. The huge open space of the main nave opened out into a broad transept at the point where the shrine rose, and was flanked on either side by two broad aisles. By the later Middle Ages there were altars all along both these walls, erected to the memory of individuals connected with the basilica, as well as the high altar beyond the *confessio* of the saint; there were also hundreds of gravestones set into the floor. St. Peter's could hardly have ever known the muted calm often associated with major places of worship. The hubbub created by hundreds of pilgrims who would visit the basilica each day, the excited groups pointing out the details on the paintings down the walls of the nave, the singing of offices by the canons of St. Peter's at all hours of the day, would mix with the cries from outside in the atrium as beggars and sellers of tracts and religious objects vied for the contents of the pilgrims' purses.

During his stay, the visitor to Rome would certainly go to other sites, some of Christian origin and some associated with ancient Rome. He would doubtless visit St. John Lateran. Until the end of the thirteenth century this was where the papal palace was located, and where the ever-growing business of the papal curia was carried on. The basilica, although slightly smaller than St. Peter's, was of comparable design. Again, one can imagine how its huge marble columns running down either side of the nave would focus attention on the apse with its mosaics catching and reflecting the light from candles and lamps round the high altar.

While at the Lateran the visitor would be shown the gilt bronze sculpture of a horseman, the most celebrated piece of antique sculpture to survive during the whole of the Middle Ages in the city. We know now that it represents the Emperor Marcus Aurelius, but there was room for opinion on this, and fortunately it was most commonly held to portray Constantine the Great, the first Christian emperor. The early guide-books to Rome claimed that it was Theodoric, or the representation of a hero from the days of ancient Rome, who, when the city was being besieged, rode bareback into the surrounding army and captured the enemy king. This explanation accounted for both the lack of a saddle and the gesture of the right hand. Other ancient sculpture in the city, such as the famous 'horse-tamers', the *caballi di marmo* now on the Capitol, the reliefs on the triumphal arches and other works that have since disappeared, would all have been the subject of interest for the visitor.

Without fail the pilgrim, as soon as he could, would take the route down the via Ostia past the pyramid of Gaius Cestius, through the Porta di S. Paolo in the city walls and on down to where the huge basilica of S. Paolo rose out of the flat terrain. Here again, in spite of its distance from the *abitato* and the Leonine City, there would have been a constant mixed hubbub of noise as the streams of fellow-pilgrims, speaking all the tongues of Europe, would stream through the great doors and approach the grave of St. Paul. Reverence for this saint ran second only to that of St. Peter, and there was a famous and extensive series of frescoes on the upper walls of the basilica depicting scenes from his life. Again, large and elaborate mosaics were to be found both in the apse and (from the 14th century) on the facade; here the depiction of the saint was accompanied by his Biblical titles of ' *Vas electionis et Doctor gentium*' (the chosen vessel and teacher of the Gentiles). These, and the frescoes, would certainly have been the subject of lingering discussion and admiration after the main purpose of the journey, the prayer and alms-giving at the apostle's tomb, had been accomplished. Travelling on foot, the visit to S. Paolo would have taken the best part of a day, such are the distances involved.

After these obligatory visits, and probably a further one to the other great Early Christian basilica of Sta. Maria Maggiore, the medieval pilgrim would have been able to follow more various interests elsewhere in the city. The great majority of visitors would have been unlearned and largely illiterate, and these would have been content to be led round the main monuments by a member of their group who knew a little classical history. Of these we have virtually no record other than their reflected views in the pilgrims' guides. The few visitors with informed learning to guide them have from time to time left us some echo of where they would have spent at least some of their time. One of the most eloquent and sensitive of these was the poet Petrarch. Although untypical in both his learning and his poetic insight and imagination, we can perhaps allow Petrarch to speak for the many visitors to Rome during the later Middle Ages who brought to their view of the city an educated and sympathetic vision. In one of his most excited and evocative passages, the poet is here writing to an old friend, a Dominican monk, Giovanni Colonna di San Vito; he is recalling the long rambles that they had taken together round the city, and it is interesting that he nowhere speaks of the glories of the mosaics of Sta. Prassede or the majesty of the basilica of S. Paolo - it was for him the antique past of Rome that held most fascination. This letter was written about 1340:

"You and I would wander through the city, so great that it feels as if it were empty in spite of its huge population. We walked not just in the city itself, but round it as well, and at every step we came upon something to stimulate our minds, and which we would discuss.... Here is the Sacred Way, and here the Esquiline hill, and the Viminal, and the Quirinal, and the Caelian; here is the Campo Marzio, and here the hand of [Tarquinius] Superbus cut off the poppy-heads. Here it was that the unhappy woman Lucretia fell on a sword to avoid her violation, and Brutus avenged his honour.... There is the bridge which is now called after St. Peter.... Here it once snowed on the fifth of August, here a stream of oil flowed into the Tiber, here, according to the legend, the Sybil showed the infant Christ to the emperor Augustus in his old age.... And when we were tired by our long walks around the city, we would often retire to the Baths of Diocletian, and even climb on to the roof of the building that had once been so splendid, because nowhere else could we get such clean air, such a good view, or such silence."

This letter gives us a fascinating glimpse into the mind of a cultivated scholar at the end of the Middle Ages. We can picture him with his Franciscan friend animatedly re-creating for themselves the heroic past of Rome; they would know the legend of Tarquinius Superbus who, as a hint to a messenger sent him by his son, cut off the heads of all the tallest poppies in his garden, which led to his son then putting to death or banishing all the leading men in the city to which he had fled. Later, Lucretia, either violated by his son, or (as Petrarch knew it) in order to escape his attentions, killed herself. The legend of snow falling in summer refers to the traditional site of the foundation of Sta. Maria Maggiore, that of the oil flowing into the Tiber harks back to the day of Christ's birth when, it was said, this miracle occurred at a building on the site of the church of Sta. Maria in Trastevere, and it was on the Capitol that the emperor Augustus was held to have been shown the infant Christ by the Sybil when he was 64.

It is clear that the sights of medieval Rome acted as a stepping-off point for much excited speculation and recounting of remote legends. It is as if the more recent buildings had not yet accrued a sufficient history or mythology of their own to be worth mentioning. Petrarch could picture with his friend the precise events of remote pre-Republican Roman history, but the towers of the Frangipani are not even mentioned. It is priorities like this that have been the cause of an evident neglect by successive ages of the great achievements of medieval Rome.

And so, as every traveller said his farewells to the city, and took a last look at the Pantheon and the Colosseum, and paid a last visit to St. Peter's, and caught his last glimpse of the forest of towers as he took the road home, what would have been the impression that he took with him? The answer might vary in some respects depending on the period of his visit. The ninth- and tenth-century pilgrim would have been more conscious of the giant remains of antiquity, and there would certainly have been more of these to see than there was in the twelfth and thirteenth century, when much had been destroyed or altered. The shift in population from the *disabitato* towards the Tiber bend and the Leonine city would have been far less advanced in the age of the first Holy Roman Emperors, and the papal curia at the Lateran would have been far less developed. But the great basilicas, which were, after all, the main focus of Christian devotion throughout the Middle Ages, would have been subject to only minimal change. If Charlemagne could have returned in the thirteenth century to the scene of his coronation in St. Peter's, he would have been conscious of many more minor altars and tombs, and probably an increase in painted decoration, as well as more mosaics on the facade, but in its main forms, the focus of Western Christendom would have been seen to have weathered the centuries without much more than essential repairs to the fabric. The builders of the fourth and fifth centuries had achieved an extraordinarily permanent solution to the needs of Rome and her population.

III The Papacy and the Cardinalate

"Thou art Peter, and upon this rock I will build my church." It is on these words, the most fundamental of the three 'Petrine texts' of the New Testament, that the claims of the Roman papacy to being the figurehead of the one true church have always rested. But between the origins of this office and the reality as it exists today, lies an enormous tract of time during which it has undergone innumerable changes and vicissitudes. It was pre-eminently during the medieval centuries that the changes took place which gave to the papacy most of the characteristics which the office still bears. Certainly, it is impossible to write a book about Medieval Rome without a discussion of this unique institution.

Two features concerning the reality of the papacy should be mentioned at once: while this chapter is going to be concerned with how this office, as it developed, impinged on the life and existence of Rome in the Middle Ages, it is impossible to confine oneself to such a subject without constantly referring to individual popes. So while it has been claimed that by virtue of Christ's words to Peter, as well as later proof, the papacy had always existed as an abstract concept, the fact remains that it was always vested in individual people, and these individuals were subject to the same range of worldly limitations as any other person in a position of authority. These limitations might be imposed by external forces, or they might be limitations of personal ability and character, but they were inevitably present throughout the development of the papacy. As we shall see, there were, during the Middle Ages, all kinds of popes: strong men and weak men, popes who were saints and popes who were sinners, some who were men of immense administrative ability and some who were inept and self-indulgent, popes who were brilliant lawyers and scholars and feeble popes who had no grasp of their potential authority. Yet they were all popes, occupying the throne of St. Peter, and heirs to the accumulated tradition of papal principles.

This leads to a second aspect which is still to be found in much of the writing on the papacy. This concerns a preconception about the office that has been widely held for centuries, and takes the form of an assumption that the papacy has always been consistently working towards some abstract aim of absolute power and universally regarded authority. This policy was always pursued as if it were some pre-ordained programme. As we shall see, the papacy, and the popes who were the embodiment of it, were reacting to whatever events and pressures their age produced. The form and extent of their reaction, was the result of the actions of the particular individual in whom the office was at the time invested. While certain general trends clearly existed, and may have persisted over quite long periods, the idea of some master-plan being followed from earliest times cannot be sustained.

For anyone in western Europe at any point in the Middle Ages there could never have been any question about the origins of the papacy: the first pope had been St. Peter, who, by virtue of the famous words quoted above, as well as the 'Charge to Peter' (the term for Christ's command to Peter, 'Feed my sheep') had been made divinely responsible by Christ for the care of the 'one holy, catholic and apostolic church'. The *'Liber Pontificalis'*, or 'Book of the Popes' recorded throughout the Middle Ages the actions of all the popes. It opens with the unambiguous statement that the first pope was St. Peter, that he was Bishop of Antioch for seven years, and he then came to Rome, and *'sedit cathedram episcopatus ann. XXV m. II d. III'* (i.e. he sat on the bishop's throne for 25 years, two months and three days) and ordained two bishops, Linus and Cletus; these were his successors on the bishop's throne in Rome. This is not the place to rehearse the arguments as to the historical evidence for St. Peter's presence in Rome (or, for that matter, that of St. Paul), or for St. Peter's martyrdom there in about 67 AD. Most modern scholars accept this as substantially correct. What is important is that for the medieval world it had the absolute certainty of historical truth, supported both by scripture and by divine revelation.

But for the modern scholar the facts are far less certain, and for the first three centuries there is more conjecture than historical truth; even to the end of the first millennium of the life of the papacy there still remain substantial questions to which no certain answer can be given. A number of important stages in the development of the medieval papacy can be established, however, and some of these should be given here so that the later overwhelming effect of the institution on the city can be assessed.

Originally, as even the '*Liber Pontificalis*' recognized, the pope was no more than the bishop of Rome. To that extent he was just one among many of the Mediterranean leaders of Christian communities, such as Alexandria, Antioch, Ephesus and even Jerusalem. The supremacy of one of these churches over any or all of the others only became a subject of debate when varieties of interpretation of the Christian faith began to emerge. Some form of authority was then needed to establish and enforce an acceptable orthodoxy. For this authority to carry sufficient weight, the concept of the 'apostolic succession' was developed, whereby a community of Christians who could claim that their foundation stemmed from one of the original apostles sent out by Christ, and could produce evidence for their claim, could legitimately feel that their interpretation was the correct one. Rome, by reason of the explicit 'charge to Peter', and other Biblical evidence such as the donation of the 'keys of heaven and of hell' to Peter, could from the start be seen to have some of the most substantial claims for the authority to decide on questions of doctrine.

But there is, of course, a very big difference between merely claiming to be an authoritative source for apostolic truth, and claiming the right to universal jurisdiction in all religious matters. This was only to emerge gradually as the medieval centuries passed. It could have been expected that when, under the emperor Constantine, Christians were finally allowed freedom of worship, the bishopric of Rome might have been given some official pre-eminence. But this does not seem to have happened; in fact the famous Edict of 313 was issued in Milan, which was at the time the capital. It is clear that the actual concept of the papacy, as it was later to emerge, simply did not exist in the early fourth century. As it was, the bishop of Rome was given in 312 an official residence by Constantine; this was a palace at the Lateran, which was to remain the palace of the popes throughout the Middle Ages.

With hindsight it is clear that the establishment of the bishop of Rome in an official residence by the emperor was a factor of enormous importance for the future of the city, but at the time this would not have been evident. It was actually in the bishopric of Milan, under the brilliant leadership of St. Ambrose, that real thought was given to the potential of a church united with a strong temporal power. It is interesting to speculate what might have happened to Rome if Milan had claimed apostolic succession superior, or at least equal, to that of Rome in the fourth century, when these developments were in progress.

The effect on Rome of Constantine's actions would have been evident at once, however. The transference of the Lateran palace was made to the bishop Miltiades, and two years later his successor, Sylvester began to build the Lateran basilica beside it; by the end of the fourth century there were probably over thirty basilicas to be seen in the city. Yet it was not until the very end of the century that we find the first bishop of Rome using the term 'pope'; he was called Siricius (384-399). During the fifth century further papal claims were initiated. Innocent I (401-417) expressed the view that any important religious matters should be referred to him, and that his decisions affected all the other churches in the world. Later fifth-century popes reiterated this view, describing the position of the church of Rome as like the head to the other parts of a body. It is clear that these claims were being made in order to maintain the position of Rome which was, by then, struggling to retain its authority with respect to the 'New Rome' founded by Constantine on the Bosphorus, and endowed with his name. This is not the place to expand on the long story of the gradual division of the Eastern and Western churches which was finally completed in the eleventh century. It is important to note that Rome was beginning to exhibit features of the later primacy that was to be claimed by the See of Rome. As was so often the case, it was not internal events which encouraged this tendency, but rather external forces.

Already under Damasus I (366-384) there is evidence that the bishop of Rome was having to assert his claims by reference to association with St. Peter; the 'Petrine tradition' in Rome was first officially put forward at a synod in Rome in 382. But if Damasus could be said to have laid the doctrinal foundations of papal primacy, it was Leo I (440-461) who, as we saw in the first chapter, was the first of the popes to represent Rome and the Roman people to an outside force when he went to talk with Attila. It must to some extent have been his personal approach to his office that brought him to this position. He saw himself, and the office of the papacy, as being by right of princely rank, and quite specifically *ruling* the See of St. Peter. The fact that he came from an ancient and aristocratic branch of the Counts of Tusculum must also have affected his attitude when he came to the papal office. Certainly he is rightly called 'Leo the Great'; after him the papacy would never be the same again.

Just as it was the rise of the patriarchate of Constantinople, to the east, and the barbarian invasions from the north, coupled with the increasing weakness of imperial power in Italy as a whole, that was to push the papacy so far up the road towards its later claims to primacy and plenitude of power, so it was external events that extended papal authority in later centuries. The expansion of the Lombards from the north, and the explosion of Islam in the east were both to have direct effects on Rome. As we have seen, Gregory I (590-604), who had seen secular office as prefect of Rome, was to become the sole and undisputed political leader who negotiated his own terms with the Lombards, again inevitably identifying the universal papal office with the city itself. It was also Gregory (later rightly called 'The Great') who was the first of the popes to make particular efforts to extend Christianity to other parts of Europe. In 596 the mission that he sent to evangelize Britain landed in Kent, and what was later to become the See of Canterbury was founded. It was then that the eventual world-wide authority of the Church of Rome could be said to have begun.

Enough has already been said to show how the respective fates of the papacy and the city of Rome were inevitably inter-twined in an ever-changing and complex web. When Leo IV commanded a fleet that succeeded in defeating the Saracens off Ostia in 849, he was by then only marginally extending a role that other popes of centuries earlier had already carved out. In each case, popes were just responding to events in the way that seemed most appropriate at the time. It is worth mentioning, though, that for the first few centuries of its existence the papacy was far from being the Italian institution that it was later to become. While many popes were naturally natives of the city itself, there was no tradition that the church of Rome should be governed by Romans. Several earlier popes came from Greece, and Miltiades was from Africa; Hilary (461-468) came from Sardinia, as did Symmachus (498-514), and the seventh and eighth centuries saw a string of Syrian or Greek popes on the throne of St. Peter. As the office of the pope came under the control of the emperor, it became common for German bishops to be elevated to the Roman See; Leo IX (1049-1054) was from Germany, as was his successor, Victor II. There was even one English pope, Nicholas Breakspeare, from Bedmond in Herefordshire, who became Hadrian IV in 1154. While the concept of nations was still far in the future, the particular tensions that a pope from outside Rome could either arouse or allay must always have played a part in the selection process.

As the papacy became more and more important as the centuries passed, it began to matter more and more who the pope was, and what it was that formed his aspirations and inclinations. As the office grew in European stature, it became increasingly common for popes to leave Rome for long periods; the claim to world-wide authority, as opposed to simply presiding over the turbulent political life of a medieval city, increasingly occupied the popes with non-Roman and non-Italian affairs. It was indeed Leo IX who brought a reforming zeal and vision to his office, and is credited with being the effective founder of the concept of the 'papal monarchy'. Coming from the north, he saw more clearly than any Roman the possibilities in the office for establishing a supra-national moral force, which could arbitrate dispassionately on questions of doctrine without regard to local political consequences. His period of office lasted for five years, but in that time he only spent some six months in Rome itself; he was absent, making the papacy an effective power outside Italy. As one of the great reforming popes he did much to restore the prestige of a church, many of whose members had become a subject of scandal in their abuse of their office and for their general moral laxity.

It is ironic that the expansion in the role and authority of the papacy during much of the medieval period was based on a deliberate forgery. At some point during the eighth or ninth centuries a document was drawn up which claimed that the emperor Constantine had conferred on Pope Sylvester I not only the primacy of the See of Rome over those of Constantinople, Jerusalem, Antioch and Alexandria, but also dominion over all of Italy, including, of course, Rome; the pope and his successors were the supreme judges of all the clergy, who themselves were granted some secular authority as well. This document became known as the Donation of Constantine, and was completely accepted throughout the Middle Ages, both by the popes and by their opponents. It was referred to again and again during the period, and was of course the basis for papal claims to authority in the city of Rome. It was only in the fifteenth century that the learned cardinal, Nicholas of Cusa, exposed it as a complete fabrication.

Of great importance to the development of Rome in the Middle Ages was the territory over which the popes were held to have a ruler's control, the so-called 'Lands of St. Peter'. Although there were periods when the popes exercised this temporal sovereignty over huge and widespread areas of Europe, including parts of France, Corsica, Sicily and Sardinia and even part of North Africa, as well as vast tracts of Italy, it is with the area round Rome that we should be most concerned. Apart from the forged Donation of Constantine, there were genuine claims to sovereignty over certain areas that had been bestowed on the papacy by, for example, the Lombard king, Liutprand, and by King Pepin. Of most importance to the Romans would have been the territory immediately round Rome, and this was continually subject to change. For the most part the tendency was for this area to contract, with the duchies of Spoleto, Naples, Tuscany or Urbino ever on the watch for a chance to expand at the expense of the 'Patrimony of St. Peter'. But while the pope could draw financial and material aid for his own purposes from these lands, the use to which they were put might conflict with the aims of the Roman people. The *Patrimonium Petri* became in this way another bone of contention over which much blood was spilt during the long medieval centuries.

But consolidation and extension of the powers and authority of the papacy continued despite changes in the territory of the papal states. Again, it tended to be external forces that were the ultimate reason for these periods of expansion. For example, it could be said that apart from the evangelizing outlook of some of the popes (such as Gregory the Great), a 'foreign policy' of the papacy did not exist; the church affairs of Rome and central Italy were a sufficient preoccupation. The overwhelming strength of Islam in the east, which by the eleventh century had complete occupation of the Holy Land, provided just the impetus for one of the great popes of the Middle Ages to see a genuine cause to which his office could be put. Gregory VII (1073-1085) had been a fiery, passionate but tactless individualist. Although a very gifted man, who had risen to the greatest position the church could offer from the humble origins of a Tuscan farm, his headstrong attempts at uniting the major European powers with the objectives of the papacy had largely failed. His effective successor, Urban II (1088-1096), was a completely different man; an astute and highly educated French nobleman, he saw that political unity was to be achieved not by confrontation but by more careful and diplomatic means. His great achievement was the organization and launching of the First Crusade, in which all the major forces of Europe, except the German imperial power, were united in a Christian war to recover the Holy Land from the infidel. The First Crusade of 1096 has been called 'the foreign policy of the reformed papacy', and it did indeed give most of Europe a common aim. It is all the more remarkable an achievement in that it was largely prepared not from Rome, where Urban could not at first enter on account of the forces of an antipope, Clement III, but from France. The Crusade strengthened his position and allowed him to return to Rome, now the moral leader of a Europe that was more united than it had been for centuries.

Urban's reign is a good example of how world-wide political events could all have a substantial effect on the city of Rome. For the pope's return there just before the launching of the Crusade made it the centre of even greater diplomatic activity. This was caused not just by the new policies involved with the Crusade, but by the huge administrative reforms that Urban began at once to institute in the government of the church. Other popes in the eleventh century had tried hard to impose reforms on unco-operative and often remote dioceses in other countries, but had been unable to monitor or enforce reform when the papal direct-

St. Maria Maggiore: apse mosaic - detail: angels and the kneeling figure of Pope Nicholas IV. (Pl. 13)

St. Maria Maggiore: apse mosaic - detail: the Dormition of the Virgin. (Pl. 14)

A late 13th century Roman panel painting of St. Lucy. (Pl. 15)

Engraved aerial view of Rome made in the later 16th century. (Pl. 16)

Sta. Maria in Aracoeli: tomb of Cardinal Matteo d'Acquasparta, with fresco by Pietro Cavallini (c. 1302). (Pl. 17)

Sta. Cecilia in Trastevere: ciborium over the high altar by Arnolfo di Cambio, dated 1293. (Pl. 18)

Sta. Cecilia in Trastevere: detail of fresco of the Last Judgement by Pietro Cavallini (late 13th century). (Pl. 19)

ives had been transmitted. Urban saw that the church lacked an effective machinery of government that was equal to the tasks of controlling what was now a world-wide organization.

The effects of Urban's reform of the church's government would have been felt at once in Rome. Not only would there have been an increase in the administrative machinery at the Lateran palace, with offices multiplying and greater numbers of personnel involved than ever before, but there would have been a greater number of visitors to the papal court, which would now hear legal cases of all kinds. All these extra numbers at the papal offices would have required the services of lodging, feeding and stabling for their horses. It is now impossible to know with any precision the numbers involved in the papal government of the church, but it is easy to make out a case for the employment of several hundred individuals, and these in turn would have depended on the supporting services of as many again. It is only necessary to visualize the problems of governing an organization stretching from Scandinavia to Sicily, controlling doctrine, appointments to church offices, collecting financial dues, initiating building programmes, and all the other day-to-day features of the government of what would now be called an international corporation, to realize the scale of the problem. To this must be added the sheer labour concerned with the writing of every single document and its copies by an individual papal scribe, on carefully prepared parchment. Copies of the correspondence for a few months can take up some four hundred pages in the papal registers. And each missive could of course only be carried by hand, and at the pace of a horse. Even a modern bureaucracy with its resources of advanced technology and banking would find this a daunting task.

The reforms of Urban provided a platform on which all later popes were able to build. During the twelfth century the legal services of the papal court were extended enormously, until it became for many types of case the supreme arbiter. The authority of the pope was so great that his decision would be sought, and respected, on a vast range of legal matters. These cases were not requested by the pope, but brought to him in their hundreds.

It can be seen that these changes in the functions of the papacy would inevitably have wide repercussions. All the greatest of the popes up to the twelfth century had had real claims to a spiritual authority, and had usually been men of outstanding spiritual gifts. None of the most effective popes of the twelfth century had pretensions to saintliness; they tended to be lawyers, often very good lawyers, but not men of genuine religious insight. Alexander III (1159-1181), and the great pope Innocent III (1198-1216), as well as the short-lived Gregory VIII were all lawyers by training, and would have spent a substantial proportion of their time acting as judges in legal cases.

This involvement of the church with the legal world was regretted by many, but was to a considerable extent an inevitable result of developments started long before. The managerial skills that the government of the church was increasingly to demand were often to be found in a legally-trained mind. For the rest of the Middle Ages all the most effective popes were to be men of the world, men at home in the field of international diplomacy; some of them were outstanding financiers. It is commonly accepted that the zenith of the medieval church was reached in the papacy of Innocent III; the particular gifts that he brought to his office were not so much concerned with religious or spiritual insight as with brilliance of intellect and power of reason, allied with supreme administrative skill. Under him, as we saw earlier, Rome came closer to being the Rome of the Caesars than it had ever been since the fifth century. The fact that the Fourth Crusade had, in 1204, placed a western ruler on the throne of Constantinople, meant that Rome could confidently claim to be *caput mundi* when the Fourth Lateran Council assembled there in 1215.

It should not be forgotten, however, that the growth and power of the papacy had quite distinct limits. While papal decisions in matters of law, and papal authority in ecclesiastical affairs, were respected all over the known world, the pope simply did not have the means to enforce all his wishes when it came to more secular matters. His final weapon was excommunication, but as an instrument of government this was simply inadequate; it tended to be either too strong, or not strong enough. So that while the medieval papacy was at its glorious height in the early thirteenth century, not only did the autocratic king John of England spend almost four years in a state of excommunication, but the entire kingdom of England was for all this time under a papal interdict; no Communion, no marriages, no investitures, no coronation - not even Christian burials were permitted. Only baptism and the last rites for the dying were allowed. Yet not once was it ever suggested that papal authority be disregarded; the pope's moral authority was still absolute, and his punishments were accepted as the price that had to be paid for taking a certain course of action.

There is one episode that illustrates very well how the character of the papacy and the individuals who filled the office had changed since the early centuries. By the late thirteenth century there was widespread discontent at the worldliness of the popes, and a yearning for a return to more spiritual values. It was the same feeling of malcontent in the previous century that had provided Arnold of Brescia with such a large following among the citizens of Rome, but we saw what his fate had been: first excommunication by the pope, and then execution by the emperor. When Nicholas IV died in 1292, however, the revulsion at the deep involvement of the papacy in secular matters was genuinely felt by a much wider range of people, which included the highest church dignitaries. It was not that the popes of the thirteenth century had been bad men; on the contrary, they were without exception men of considerable education and each, in his own way, of some real personal distinction. Only Boniface VIII, at the close of the century, was to be notorious for personal immorality. It was simply that the huge government machine erected by the church was overwhelming all of them with its complexity and weight of detail. Although Gregory X (1271-1276) was a religious and reformatory pope and made a substantial contribution to European political and religious problems, he failed to make a lasting impression. He was elected pope only after a vacancy of three years, during which agreement could not be reached on a suitable candidate. The same agonizing indecision must have gone on in 1292, and was compounded by the college of cardinals being split into two factions, headed by the rival Roman families of the Orsini and the Colonna.

In the end, after two years of bitter deadlock, the cardinals elected, as Celestin V, a man of nearly 80 who had spent his entire adult life as an ascetic hermit in the wilds of the Abruzzi. He was called Pietro da Morrone, and he could not have been a more complete contrast to the concept of a pope as it had developed during the previous century. Completely unworldly, naive to the point of simplicity, he was a man of saintly meekness of spirit. His pontificate was short and absolutely disastrous. He would sign any document which was put before him, and became a mere tool in the hands of Charles II of Naples, so alienating all the supporters who had hoped for a new set of priorities in the papal rule. Completely ignorant of ceremonial, Celestin was miserable amid the luxuries of court life and soon yearned for the simple solitude that he had left behind.

The lessons to be learnt from the bizarre episode of Celestin V were certainly not lost on those charged with the election of later popes. Never again was it thought that the only quality that a pope should possess was saintliness of character. For better or worse, it was now essential that popes be men of the world, good managers, and (if possible) good financiers; these qualities tended to be foremost in all the most successful popes of the later Middle Ages. Good lawyers were now less common, and personal sanctity of life or spirituality of outlook could usually only be found lower down the church's hierarchy.

But it is time to turn from the subject of the papacy itself to that of the pope's immediate court, and in particular the cardinals, who came to play an increasingly important role, both in the affairs of the church and of Rome itself. Like any lay ruler, the popes developed an official entourage of advisers that has sometimes been compared to the function of a senate. Like the papacy itself it grew in response to the needs for such a body. As the functions of the papacy became more complex and widespread, so the court of the pope expanded in importance and the range of interests over which it exercised its care. From the moment when we begin to hear of this court until the end of the Middle Ages, it is composed of officials known as cardinals, and again the fact that the pope was the Bishop of Rome is significant in the way that the cardinalate developed.

It is perhaps surprising that it is not until the eighth century, in the pontificate of Stephen III (752-757), that mention is first made of seven 'cardinal bishops'; to these were later added cardinal-priests, who were parish priests of various Roman churches, and cardinal-deacons, who had care of the poor in the seven districts of Rome. So it can be seen that the cardinalate began as a kind of council for the bishop of Rome, specifically based in the city. This 'parochial' aspect of the cardinalate could not last the growing internationalism of the church, and by the eleventh century there were cardinals being appointed from countries north of the Alps to increase the breadth of the counsel that the pope needed. While the pope always retained the absolute power of a monarch, in that he could claim succession from none less than St. Peter, the story of the medieval cardinalate is one of ever-increasing importance and influence. It was, for example, because Charles II, King of Naples, wanted to have a substantial faction within the *Curia* (or court) sympathetic to his interests that, during the episode of Celestin V's reign mentioned above, he persuaded him to appoint twelve new cardinals, all of whom were the king's nominees. Seven of them were Frenchmen, and one was even the king's own chancellor.

The importance of the cardinals lay, of course, in the fact that it was they who selected the pope's successor. In the interval after a pope's death, the government of the church actually devolved solely upon the college of cardinals. As the papacy grew in importance, so naturally did the cardinalate. Their numbers varied considerably during the medieval period, only being fixed at seventy as late as 1586. For most of the Middle Ages there were much fewer than this, with many elections being decided by twenty cardinals or less. As the importance of the papacy increased, tight controls over elections were introduced. Surprisingly, it was not until the Third Lateran Council of 1179 that the right to elect a pope was specifically restricted to existing cardinals, and it was only then that the need for a two-thirds majority was laid down.

Unlike a dynastic succession, it was open to the cardinals to select whoever they wanted to be the next pope. They were not obliged to choose one of their own number, and quite frequently chose an individual who was not already a cardinal. In rare cases someone who was not even a priest or monk might receive the necessary majority. Under these conditions, it might be thought surprising, with the ability and brains of the entire known world at the cardinals' disposal, that all the popes were not men of outstanding brilliance. Yet it was because the pope's position continued to be of such increasing importance that political considerations so often prevented what might otherwise have been the best decision from being made. On some occasions, when agreement was clearly going to be impossible, the cardinals appointed a small sub-committee to make a choice for them. This was the case in 1265, when after a vacancy of four months following the death of Urban IV, the college of cardinals left the decision to two of their number. The outcome was the election of a Frenchman, Guy Foulques, as Clement IV.

The reasons for these long struggles to arrive at an agreement are not hard to find. While it might be thought that as the cardinals were appointed by the popes, and the popes were elected by the cardinals, there might be the basis for a relatively stable range of policies to be pursued. Yet Roman, or Italian, political life never provided the background for such stability, and time and again it can be seen that one pope was elected as a reaction against the extremes of his predecessor, or in response to contrary conditions.

One of the longest vacancies in the history of the papacy occurred after the death of Clement IV in 1268, and this offers a good example of the weaknesses of the system. One of the principal reasons for the long delay was the rivalry between the French and Italian groups among the cardinals, and so long as there was no pope, the French king, Charles of Anjou, had the political field largely to himself, and so had an interest in prolonging the vacancy as long as possible. The cardinals met, broke up, re-met, and the months dragged on into years. In the summer of 1271 they met in Viterbo to avoid the fever and heat of Rome, when the local populace became so enraged at the endless delay in giving the world another pope that they stripped the roof off the palace where the cardinals were meeting, in order to force a decision. The *Curia* then agreed to leave the decision to six of their number, who chose Tebaldo Visconti. He was at the time in the Holy Land, but on his return was crowned pope as Gregory X.

The scandalous delay which preceded his election prompted Gregory to formulate the idea of the *conclave*, when the cardinals were literally locked up. There was to be a period of only ten days after the death of a pope before the election of his successor began. If all the cardinals could not be brought back in time, this could not be helped. Each was to appear with just a single servant in the palace of the dead pope, and they were to live there all together in the same room. The doors and windows would then be walled up, with just one opening left for food to be passed in. If a new pope had not been elected within three days, the cardinals' food was to be reduced to two dishes a day for the next five days, and after that to a diet of bread, water and wine only. It is certainly hard to imagine another three-year vacancy occurring under these conditions, and although they were suspended quite soon, they were brought back later, and remain the basis of the conclave to the present day.

The later thirteenth century saw the importance of the college of cardinals reach its high point for the whole of the Middle Ages. The growing influence that they had on the affairs of the papacy, and so indirectly on European politics, was acknowledged in a decree of Nicholas of 1289. In it he allotted to the cardinals half of all the revenues that came to the pope from all over Europe. While this would allow only a fraction to each cardinal, if there were ten of them, then each would receive only a twentieth. In any case, many of them were already wealthy men in their own right. Two of the cardinals in 1289 were members of the very wealthy Orsini family, and two were of the Colonna, while two more that were to be added to the college were Gaetani. There must have been a number of cases of cardinals having more money to spend on expensive projects of their own choosing, such as buildings and forms of artistic patronage, than the pope, whose resources (albeit much greater) were often needed for political or even military requirements. Certainly the people of Rome would have been used to seeing many of the cardinals living in very considerable luxury, with large, richly-supplied households, and their spending would have been spread over a wide range of the city's services.

It would seem appropriate to close this chapter with a description of a papal coronation; this would be the one moment when the deliberations of the college of cardinals, meeting in their conclave, would take physical shape in a show of magnificent ecclesiastical splendour, as the new pope was shown to the world. In the traditions of the papal coronation, the close links of the papacy, not just with the city of Rome but also with the Roman people, were always given the clearest expression. To whatever extent the pope might become a figure on the international stage, at that special moment he belonged to Rome, and embodied the aspirations of all Romans for the religion given them by St. Peter.

There are descriptions of the ceremonies of papal processions from the twelfth century, and they undoubtedly reflect earlier usage. It is clear that the occasion of a coronation was one of great rejoicing and festivity, with whole streets being decorated for the pope to traverse on his way to or from St. Peter's. The route of the procession was arranged so that the majority of the Roman people had the chance to see the new pope. As we have seen, there was a complicated love-hate relationship between the popes and the medieval populace of Rome. Although they were immeasurably proud of the pope as their figurehead, their love could quickly turn to vindictive antagonism if he failed them. The ceremonies of the coronation, with the pope throwing handfuls of coins to the crowds as they cheered him along the processional route, were expressive of their mutual need for each other's support.

Although there are earlier descriptions of the coronation processions from official sources such as the *Liber Censuum*, they tend to be rather factual, giving lists of the streets through which the pope would pass, first on his way to St. Peter's, and then back to his palace at the Lateran. The account given here is actually from the year 1404, when the popes had returned from Avignon; by now their home was in the Vatican palace, whereas earlier popes had lived at the Lateran, and so had a much longer journey to make through Rome. The description which follows was written by a British cleric, Adam of Usk, and although he saw details that were clearly additions to older ceremonies, his account captures well the excitement and significance of what was then already an ancient ritual.

"On the feast of St. Martin (11th November) the new pope went down from the palace to the church of St. Peter for the ceremony of his coronation, and at the altar of St. Gregory, the auditors bringing the vestments, he was robed for the Mass. And, at the moment of his coming forth from the chapel of St. Gregory, the clerk of his chapel, bearing a long rod on the end of which was fixed some tow, cried aloud as he set it aflame: 'Holy father, thus passeth away the glory of the world'; and again, in the middle of the procession, with a louder voice, thus twice: 'Holy father! Most holy father!'; and a third time, on arriving at the altar of St. Peter, thrice: 'Holy father! Holy father! Holy father!' at his loudest; and forthwith each time the tow is quenched. Just as in the coronation of the emperor, in the very noontide of his glory, stones of every kind and colour, worked with all the cunning of the craft, are wont to be presented to him by the stone-cutters, with these words: 'Most excellent prince, of what kind of stones wilt thou that thy tomb be made?' So also the new pope, the Mass being ended by him, ascends a lofty stage made for this purpose, and there he is solemnly crowned with the triple golden crown by the cardinal of Ostia as dean of the college. The first crown betokens power in temporal things; the second, fatherhood in things spiritual; the third, grandeur in things of heaven. And afterwards, still robed in the same white vestments, he, as well as all the prelates likewise in albs, rides thence through Rome to the church of St. John Lateran, the cathedral seat proper of the pope. Then, after turning aside, out of abhorrence of Pope Joan, whose image with her son stands in stone in the direct road near S. Clemente, the pope, dismounting from his horse, enters the Lateran for his enthronement. And there he is seated in a chair of porphyry, which is pierced beneath for this purpose, that one of the younger cardinals may make proof of his sex; and then, while a 'Te Deum' is chanted, he is borne to the high altar.

"In their street the Jews offered to him their law, that is the Old Testament, seeking his confirmation; and the pope took it gently in his hands, for by it we have come to the knowledge of the Son of God and to our faith, and thus answered: 'Your law is good; but ye understand it not, for old things are passed away, and all things are become new.' And, as if for a reproach, since they being hardened in error understand it not, he delivers it back to them over his left shoulder, neither annulling nor confirming it.

"Then rode with the pope not only those of his court and the clergy, but also the thirteen quarters of the city with their captains and standards at their heads. During the progress, in order to ease the thronging of the people, largess was thrice cast among the crowd, and a passage was thus cleared while it was being gathered up.

"Now I rejoice that I was present and served in that great solemnity, as also I did in the coronation of king Henry the fourth of England and in the confirmation of the empire spoken of above."

(*Chronicon Adae de Usk*, Transl. E.M. Thompson, 1904)

Like most ancient ritual, the coronation and enthronement of the pope had gathered features down the centuries, but had probably lost very little. So that when Adam of Usk saw Cosimo de' Migliorati made pope as Innocent VII in 1404, the ceremonies would in essence have changed little for several centuries. The lighting and extinguishing of the tow three times symbolized the passing of earthly vanities. At a later date the simple lump of tow was changed to small models of castles and palaces made in wax, so making the *gloria mundi* seem even more ephemeral when they were set alight. While there had been a special papal headgear since at least the eighth century, it had had no more than one coronet until Boniface VIII added a second one at the end of the thirteenth, to symbolize the two-fold power of the papacy. The third crown was added a few years later, and was certainly present on the tiara of Clement V (1305-1314); the 'triple golden crown' which was placed on the pope's head in Adam's description, and of which he gives us the symbolism, had therefore only been in use for the relatively short period of about a century. This feature is a good example of the basic conservatism of this kind of ritual, which allowed a gradual development in some of its aspects.

The reference to the statue of 'pope Joan', which we know from other writers certainly existed near the Colosseum, relates to a curious late medieval legend, now discredited. According to this legend a woman, about the year 1100, after a distinguished career as a scholar, was eventually made pope. During a procession to the Lateran some two years after her election she actually gave birth to a baby boy, and died immediately after; the statue, holding her son, was erected between S. Clemente and the Colosseum, where the event is supposed to have occurred. This prompted the later tradition of certifying the maleness of all popes before their enthronement, the custom to which Adam refers. The popular name for the 'porphyry throne' he mentions was the *sedes probatoria* or 'seat of proof', but this name was itself probably a misunderstanding of some Latin sung during the enthronement.

The interesting reference to the meeting with the Jews goes back to the days of Innocent II (1130-1143), when this pope had to take refuge in Paris; on entering Paris the Jews presented him with a scroll of the Pentateuch, and this brief ceremony was then incorporated into the papal coronation ceremonies in Rome. The actual location of the meeting changed at least twice, being previously at the Monte Giordano and near the Castel S. Angelo, but by the fourteenth century clearly took place near the Colosseum.

The 'thirteen quarters of the city', whose representatives accompanied the papal procession, refers to the thirteen *Rioni*, or administrative districts into which the city was divided in the Middle Ages. Each of the *Rioni* still has its own emblem, and these would have appeared on flags or standards held by the elected leader of each district, presenting a marvellously colourful display. This feature, with the throwing of coins to the crowds of the Roman populace who were present, illustrates well the close bonds which tied the pope, whatever his nationality, to the city of Rome. Whether the pope liked it or not, at this moment he was seen by all the world to be inextricably linked to the See of St. Peter.

IV   The Religious Life of Rome

We have seen how Rome became established during the Middle Ages as the home and centre of the Catholic Church, and how this became one of the main unifying forces in western Europe during this period. Yet what effect did being the centre of an international religious organization have on the day-to-day religious life of its citizens? It is difficult to answer this question, for the simple reason that what is normal and ordinary tends never to be recorded in any direct sense; instead, a picture has to be built up from a wide range of more obliquely expressed evidence. In this chapter we shall try to assemble from a variety of sources some kind of composite picture of the religious life of the millions of Roman citizens of whom little individual record exists. To achieve this it will be necessary to let a few isolated voices speak to us from the past, and allow them to represent their numberless and silent fellow-citizens from the medieval centuries of Rome.

When we start to put together such a picture it soon becomes clear that the religious life of the city went on at several different levels, and that at different times these levels could change enormously in their relative importance. It might be thought, for instance, that for the mass of Roman citizens their local parish would have provided the focus of their religious life. But the concept of the parish church was surprisingly slow to develop in the Middle Ages, and only tended to become a dominant feature towards the twelfth century. (In fact, if there was one period to which all medieval Romans would hark back with pride and joy, it was that of the pre-medieval city, when Christians were martyred during the persecutions of the pagan emperors; for them, this was the heroic age of the religious life of their city.)

We could start by trying to assess the impact made on the daily life of Rome by the most substantial of the physical survivals that can still be seen in the city from the medieval period - its multitude of churches. It is a symptom of the vitality of the religious life of Rome that its churches, in particular the smaller ones, were always subject to change of all kinds: partial or complete rebuilding, extension, embellishment of all parts such as the addition or renewal of wall-paintings or mosaics, as well as periods of fluctuating fortune when finances increased or diminished as local conditions changed. While we know that this process of constant change went on in the secular buildings of the city, it is clear that the same attentions were also lavished on all church buildings while conditions allowed.

This ebb and flow of life in the churches must always have been apparent; even in the earliest period of the Christian life of the city, when during the fourth and fifth centuries the greatest of the basilicas were built, which must have completely dominated the appearance of the city, so in periods of decline they must have presented an even more telling image of gloom. Even the greatest of them was not spared. During the lean years of the papal residence in Avignon the campanile of St. Peter's was struck by lightning, and for years the damage went unrepaired, as resources and morale were both at a low ebb.

From time to time records were made of the number and identity of the churches of Rome, and it is these which give us one of the truest pictures of the religious life of the mass of the Roman citizens. The great basilicas were to a major extent the domain of the visitors to the city, but for the lay population their smaller, local church would have been the centre of their devotions. One of the most reliable and interesting of these records dates from about 1320, and gives a telling picture of the multitude of smaller churches that were then to be found in Rome. It lists a total of 414 churches in all, although all at that time were said to be in ruins, and 43 to have had no permanent clergy in charge of them. Clearly, in the preceding two centuries or so, all of these would have been in use, but the dwindling fortunes of the city while the popes were away from it, were even then beginning to show. 261 parish churches were said to be of a size to need either one or two priests for their support. It would have been these that must have served the spiritual needs of the bulk of the population of Rome at that time. One can picture the daily and weekly round of services at such modest churches as S. Giovanni Mercato ('St. John of the Market') and S. Lorenzo de Bascis, which supported only one priest, and drew its congregation from the immediate neighbourhood.

It would be in this multitude of smaller churches that the religious life of Rome would have come closest to that of any other of the major medieval cities of Europe. The entire existence of every citizen, from the cradle, when baptism would have been administered within a few days of birth, through the rhythms of daily, weekly and yearly services, to the day of their death, when they were finally laid to rest in one of the medieval city burial-grounds, was lived within a framework provided by their religion. The devotions of the churches of Rome would have included all the traditional feasts of the Christian year as the day for their commemoration came round, but there would have been some feasts which called for special celebration, as they were closely related to Roman events. For example, on 6th May there would have been a special feast-day in honour of St. John, who by tradition had survived an attempted martyrdom by boiling him in oil by the 'Latin Gate' into Rome. All Roman churches would have celebrated this feast, but for the church of S. Giovanni ad Portam Latinam, which had been built on the site of this event, it would have been one of the most precious days of the year. The medieval frescoes which can still be seen today on its walls would have looked down on its local congregation as they kept this as one of their principal holy days. The celebration of the patronal feast of any church would have been in this way the subject for annual local services of particular importance.

There is one feature of the religious life of Rome that would have marked every day for each single citizen, and that is the sound of its church bells. We have already seen how a number of medieval campaniles, usually standing slightly apart from the main church building, can still be found in the city; in many cases they are the only part of the medieval fabric of a church that has not since been altered. In a period when timepieces of any kind would have been extremely rare, the sound of the bells ringing from these campaniles would have been the only way of giving a regular and measured structure to the day-to-day life of the neighbourhood. The perpetual presence of the sound of church bells must have given them an importance that it is hard to exaggerate; they would not only have been the signal for the start of daily services in each parish church, but convents and monasteries, too, would have used them. Events such as the marriages and deaths of parishioners would also have been signalled by bells, as would moments of danger or crisis. On major feast days, as scores of churches celebrated the occasion, their bells would clang out over the roofs of the buildings of the *abitato* in a way that would have surely been both unforgettable and integral to Roman life.

The parochial life of the majority of Roman citizens - in the sense of their 'belonging' to a parish church by reason of where they happened to live - may well have been less tightly organized than in other cities. As parochial organization grew more closely controlled during the eleventh and twelfth centuries, it is possible that as Rome was such an international centre of pilgrimage the usual strictures were less rigidly enforced. For the rest of Europe the parish became an extraordinarily self-contained unit. For example, parish priests were not allowed to baptize or marry anyone from a strange parish, and the Lateran Council of 1215 made it obligatory for every parishioner to make confession at least once a year to his parish priest, and to no other. Confession could be made to someone else only by genuine travellers, and by those on the point of death. If a parish priest did not know by personal appearance one of his congregation who appeared at Mass, he could have him ejected unless he was a beggar or someone nobly born. It could be that Rome, with its constantly changing population of pilgrims, as well as the perpetual stream of visitors to the papal court, might not have been able to keep so closely to the concepts of personal knowledge of each of his flock on the part of the parish priest. And yet it is possible to find evidence for the more inward-looking qualities of parochial life that were embodied in the Lateran Council decrees. Just as a modern tourist can, in a few days of intensive sightseeing, know a city's monuments and museums better than the inhabitant who has grown up within a short distance of them, so in Rome it could be that the daily round of parish life meant that citizens would not know much outside their own restricted sphere of existence.

Certainly Petrarch was shocked at the ignorance of their city on the part of its inhabitants when he exclaimed, in a letter written to Giovanni Colonna di San Vito (in about 1340), "I say it unwillingly: nowhere is Rome less known than in Rome itself."

Another world of religious existence was lived out in the many monasteries and convents of the city. As in other aspects of the city's life, these would have been subject to constant change. During the seventh and eighth centuries, for example, due to the disturbances of the iconoclast regime in the eastern Mediterranean, there was a large influx of Greek and Syrian monks into Rome. By 650 there were Syrian monks from S. Sabbas, in the hills outside Jerusalem, settled in Rome and (though much altered) the church of S. Saba can still be seen today as evidence of their presence. Just outside Rome monks from Asia Minor had also by then settled at the site of St. Paul's execution. This was called the Tre Fontane on account of the legend that at each of the three points where the saint's head bounced a spring of water had appeared. A monastery is still there today, although staffed by Trappist monks. Colonies of Greek and Armenian monks also arrived in Rome in considerable numbers as the frontiers of Islam expanded and added to the persecutions of the iconoclasts.

But the most striking change in the religious life of the city would have occurred only from the thirteenth century, when the phenomenon of the mendicant friars swept through Italy and the rest of Europe. These were orders of monks who were forbidden to own any property in common, and so lived either by working at manual tasks or by begging; because of their way of life, they tended to be concentrated in cities, and so would have been an increasingly common sight on the streets of Rome during this century. The most famous of these orders have always been those of the Franciscans and the Dominicans - the followers of the rule of St. Francis (who had died in 1226, but whose Order had their rule approved by Honorius III in 1223) and those of St. Dominic whose Order was approved in 1216. While these monks would have been the most numerous, there were also other orders such as the Carmelites, who were given special privileges by Innocent IV in 1245. While this is not the place to go into the development of these orders, and all the tensions that grew up as a result of the internal divisions which rocked them during the period, it is certain that Rome would have seen a major change in its religious life as a direct result of the growth of the mendicant orders. Perhaps less evident to visitors, but also to be seen in this context, is the establishment of orders for women. The Poor Clares, for example, were founded by St. Francis and St. Clare, and received their first rule in 1219; in 1247 Innocent IV sanctioned the Order's second rule and its members would certainly have formed part of the population of Rome that lived a strictly enclosed life under vows of poverty, chastity and obedience. In the next century St. Bridget of Sweden was to found her Order, the Brigittines. Although the Order was based in Sweden, it is interesting that St. Bridget spent the last twenty years of her life in Rome, and suggests that she could influence the spread of her Order more readily from there than from its home base, even though the papacy was, at that time, established in Avignon.

Besides the mendicant monks and nuns, some of whom would have made a specific impact on the appearance of the city from the thirteenth century onwards, another huge mass of individuals would almost always have been present in Rome, and these were the pilgrims. Throughout the entire Middle Ages they would have been there, coming from all over the known world, variously dressed according to their country and station in life, and speaking an infinite range of languages and dialects. In particular localities of Rome they would have provided an overwhelming presence, especially at the main sites of St. Peter's and S. Paolo-fuori-le-mura, St. John Lateran and other of the main basilicas and at the main classical ruins such as the Colosseum. Specific provision was made for them in hostels and inns, many of which had a nationalistic basis, so that pilgrims would be lodging with their fellow-countrymen. It is not difficult to imagine the excited conversation as they returned to their quarters at nightfall and discussed the sights they had seen that day. For the citizens of Rome, the pilgrims would not have had any individual identity, but would be seen only as a huge, ever-changing mass of individuals. However, the economy of many parts of the city's life would have depended on them, and if their numbers dropped through reasons of political disturbance, famine or plague, countless livelihoods would have been adversely affected.

The practice of pilgrimage is based on the belief that by visiting a locality which has been hallowed by some event, or become the burial place of someone of exceptional sanctity, the pilgrim will achieve some measure of spiritual virtue or reward. There were a number of such centres of pilgrimage in Europe during the Middle Ages: Jerusalem with its holy sites, Compostela, in Spain, the traditional burial-place of St. James, and Canterbury, in England, the site of the martyrdom and tomb of St. Thomas à Becket. But among these centres, Rome was always the most venerable, housing as it did the tombs of both St. Peter and St. Paul, and at periods when travel to the Holy Land was particularly difficult, Rome was the supreme goal of all pilgrims. It is impossible to imagine the city as having an existence without this function. From the seventh and eighth centuries they would have made an increasing impact on the appearance of parts of Rome as the various national groups set up their inns and other buildings.

Almost as important to pilgrims as the tombs of the apostles were the multitudes of saints' relics of which Rome was the guardian. From the very earliest Christian times, it was accepted that the physical remains of people who had lived lives of exceptional sanctity were themselves capable of imparting virtue. Of the thousands of relics kept in Rome, pride of place seems to have gone to the 'Veronica', the handkerchief on which Christ was held to have impressed his features on the way to Calvary. This, with the relics of the birth and circumcision of Christ, and a flask of the Virgin's milk, were the most sacred of the city's relics. It is clear that it was not the living that the pilgrims came to venerate, but the dead and their physical remains. The popes, although later known as the vicars of Christ, were only the caretakers of the sacred sites and objects, and it is clear from pilgrims' accounts that these were the main focus of their devotion and religious zeal.

But above all these forms of religious life of Rome (the parochial, the monastic and the ceaseless ebb and flow of pilgrims) would have loomed the presence of the papacy and the papal court. With the pope at its head, this would have been a tightly organized and independent bureaucracy. In the earlier Middle Ages it would have made less impact on the life of the city as it was a far less elaborate and comprehensive organization, but from the eleventh century onwards, its presence would have been more and more in evidence. It is easy to take for granted the achievements of organization represented by the papal curia, but as we have seen, they were considerable. To run as relatively efficiently as it did, one must assume that, at least by the twelfth century, it had become a large and highly integrated body of men. While most of the papal business would have been concerned with affairs outside the city, the presence alone of substantial numbers of very able men involved there would have had a marked effect on the day-to-day life of many of the city's churches.

The wiser popes, however, were always careful to maintain their image with the Roman people. The pope was, after all, their bishop, and they had assisted at his coronation. There were numerous charities at work in Rome, virtually all of them ecclesiastical, and mostly for the benefit of the city's poor. In 1320, for example, we know that there were no less than 25 hospitals in operation, although some of them must have been very small, as the total number of personnel employed in them is given as 97. One of the most prominent of these hospitals was founded by Innocent III in the year of his coronation, 1198. Called the Hospital of Sto. Spirito in Sassia, it involved the merging of the church of Sta. Maria in Sassia with his new hospital. The name was derived from 'St. Mary of the Saxons', as it was located in an area near to St. Peter's which had been adopted by the 'Saxon', or English, community.

The statutes of the hospital show how Innocent wished the 'public face' of the papacy to have a genuinely charitable aspect, no doubt in contrast to the more official ways in which he usually appeared. Like most hospitals of the period, besides caring for the sick, it also provided shelter for travellers. In Rome there would always have been a stream of claimants to the papal court, as well as pilgrims and other visitors. In addition, it acted as an orphanage and foundling hospital, and ran a maternity service. There was even provision for sinful women who wished to live chastely during Holy Week, to stay there free of charge, remaining until the end of the octave of Easter, if they wished. The sisters of the hospital had to wash the heads of the sick on Tuesdays and their feet on Thursdays, and once a week had to go out into the streets of Rome to look for the homeless sick and bring them back to the hospital for care and treatment. In 1320 this exacting labour was being performed by just 30 'brothers and helpers'. A touching footnote to the devoted labours of the staff of this hospital can be found in its 'Anniversary Book', where, on 14th July every year, the name of Sister Joanna della Roccha della Vatte was remembered in the day's Masses, "who was governess of the girls of the Hospital and gave perfect service."

The most public aspect of the Hospital of Sto. Spirito in Sassia would have been the annual 'station' which Innocent III instituted for the first Sunday after the octave of the Epiphany. On that day he would come in a large procession to the Hospital, in which the most revered of all the relics in Rome, the veil of Veronica, would be carried. He would say Mass, preach a sermon and grant an indulgence to those who were present. It is interesting to note the numbers who were present for these visits, and we are able to be quite accurate about this. The pope would give three pennies each to a hundred of the poor who were already in the hospital, and the same sum to no less than a thousand of the poor of the whole city. The money was intended to buy one pennyworth each of bread, wine and meat. In medieval Rome, in the middle of winter, it is not hard to imagine the enthusiasm with which these proceedings were attended, and one can be sure that there would have been more than a thousand of the poor present, hoping to receive the pope's alms.

It would be impossible to present a picture of the religious life of late medieval Rome without some description of the phenomenon of the first Jubilee. To understand the full significance of this, something must first be said about the tradition of 'indulgences' which had been growing steadily from the late eleventh century. This was, in effect, the forgiveness of the need to do penance, or to undergo punishment for sins after confession, for a certain period. Originally this was the sole prerogative of the pope, and could only be granted by application to him in Rome. The practice became more and more common, particularly as a result of the Crusades; all those who took part in liberating Jerusalem from the infidel were even granted a 'plenary indulgence', meaning that for all the rest of their life on earth, those who had gained such an indulgence, were automatically absolved from any punishment for their sins.

In 1240 Gregory IX had announced an indulgence of three years and three 'quarantines' (each quarantine was a period of forty days) for anyone who visited the basilicas in Rome of St. Peter's and S. Paolo between the feast of Pentecost and the octave of the feast-day of these saints; but this was only regularizing and expanding a system that was already in full operation. Another world-famous source of indulgences was the sequence of the 'Forty Stations'; this involved a traditional series of the churches of Rome, in each of which the pope said Mass on each day of Lent. Towards the end of the thirteenth century, it was decreed that pilgrims to the city would receive one year and one quarantine of indulgences for attending each or any of these stations. Many pilgrims would stay in Rome for the whole of Lent, attending all forty stations, and so accumulating almost forty-five years - and this would have been increased by any extra years that could be earned at any of the many other stations.

Control over this system was hard to maintain, and by the late thirteenth century, it had begun to get out of hand. The great basilicas of Rome, which were the real centres of devotion for pilgrims, had all begun to increase their indulgences in order not to lose their popularity to the lesser churches. Nicholas IV, for example, increased the indulgence attainable at St. Peter's to seven years and seven quarantines, and later extended this to St. John Lateran and Sta. Maria Maggiore. By the end of the century, a pilgrim who spent all Lent in Rome and attended all of the forty stations as well as visiting other churches and individual altars which carried separate indulgences, could accumulate several hundred years of indulgences - enough for many life-times. It is clear that a form of inflation had set in: an inflation, it might be said, of piety. To give an idea of its runaway rate, one has only to read accounts from the 1370s when, after earning seven years' indulgence as he climbed each of the 29 steps up to St. Peter's, a pilgrim could then obtain the extraordinary period of three thousand years' indulgence by spending one hour praying at the altar of the Veronica.

It is against this background of rapidly expanding enthusiasm for Rome as the major centre of pilgrimage for the whole world that one should see the extraordinary phenomenon of the first Jubilee. It seems that this was a spontaneous idea that arose towards the end of 1299, in which, reminiscent of the Jewish Jubilee, every centennial year should be a year of special spiritual rewards, and when pilgrims to the graves of the two greatest of the apostles would be granted vast remissions.

The word spread like wildfire through Europe, and even by New Year's Eve of 1299 a great crowd had assembled at St. Peter's to greet the opening of the Jubilee Year at midnight. From then on, the crowds flocked to Rome from all over the known world. No-one had ever experienced anything like it before. The crowds were so massive that the papal police had to institute a keep-right system for all the crowds crossing the bridge on foot that led over the Tiber to St. Peter's. Dante, who was almost certainly in Rome in 1300 (and even set the *Divine Comedy* in the Holy Year of 1300) describes how ... "The Romans, because of the great throng in the year of the Jubilee, have made people pass over the bridge in such a way that on one side they face the Castle [of Sant' Angelo] and go to St. Peter's, and on the other they go toward the Mount [probably meaning the Gianicolo]. (*Inferno*, XVIII, 28 ff.)

The spontaneity and scale of the Jubilee took everyone by surprise. Even the pope, Boniface VIII, seems to have been non-plussed by it, and only issued the decree authorizing it late in February 1300. The various estimates made by contemporaries of the numbers that visited Rome vary so widely that none can be regarded as trustworthy, but it was probably somewhere between one and two million. The Florentine historian, Giovanni Villani, who visited Rome in 1300, gives a further interesting detail concerning the length of time that pilgrims spent in Rome: "Romans had to stay 30 days, everyone else 15 days, visiting the shrines of SS. Peter and Paul. They could then be granted full and entire remission of all their sins, both the guilt and the punishment thereof, they having made or to make confession of the same." By 'Romans', Villani would have meant those who lived in the Papal State, who had to stay longer because it was so much easier and cheaper for them to reach Rome.

As might be expected, an influx of such numbers caused a shortage of all the necessities of life, shelter, food and drink, and all prices increased rapidly. Here is a graphic account by a chronicler, William Ventura, who visited Rome at the end of 1300:

"It was a marvellous thing how many went to Rome in that year, for I was there and stayed for 15 days. Of bread, wine, meat, fish and fodder for horses there was, but all at special prices...Leaving Rome on Christmas Eve I saw a great crowd, that I was not able to number; there was a report among the Romans that there were then more than two million men and women in the city. Several times I saw men and women trampled under the feet of others, and even I was in the same danger, only just escaping on several occasions. The Pope received an untold amount of money from them, as day and night two priests stood at the altar of St. Paul's holding rakes in their hands, raking in infinite money...And I, William, was there, and earned fifty years and more of indulgence. Each hundred years it will be the same."

(*Chronicon Astense*, Ch. 26). Author's Transl.

One can be certain that for the citizens of Rome the spiritual blessings received and the financial rewards of providing services for the huge crowds involved, far outweighed the disadvantages of over-crowding and shortage of food. Before long there was a move to institute another Jubilee before the next one fell due in 1400. Eventually, in 1342, a delegation of thirteen Roman citizens, among which was the famous patriot Cola di Rienzo, made the journey to Avignon to ask the pope, Clement VI, if he would agree to the Jubilee being held every fifty years, with the next one falling due in 1350. They reasoned that if every person in their lifetime was to have an opportunity of receiving the spiritual benefits accruing from a visit to the Eternal City in the Jubilee Year, it was unreasonable to expect that those born not long after 1300 would still be alive in 1400. The pope agreed to their request, and issued the famous bull *Unigenitus*, using a text from Leviticus to ratify the new Jubilee: "And ye shall hallow the fiftieth year, and proclaim liberty throughout all the land unto all the inhabitants thereof: it shall be jubilee unto you." (Ch. 25, v. 10). So in 1350 the Jubilee again took place, although the pope was now far away in Avignon.

As in 1300, huge numbers flocked to Rome. Recollections and stories of the first Jubilee were clearly circulating, and some countries actually forbad their citizens to attend, on the grounds that an exodus on the scale of that of 1300 would cause a dangerous drainage of manpower at a time of wars, and that the outflow of currency would harm the economy. The numbers that came were certainly sufficient to cause many problems. Besides the shortage of supplies and consequent expense, there were again reports almost daily of pilgrims being crushed and trampled to death at points of greatest stress. One of the conditions that Clement VI had attached to the Jubilee indulgences of 1350 was that the church of St. John Lateran, as well as those of St. Peter and St. Paul, had to be visited by every pilgrim. It is an indication of the numbers that were involved that it was only possible to make the round trip of these three basilicas, which involved a distance of some eighteen kilometres, at a slow walking-pace, so dense were the crowds.

While accounts of the first Jubilee for the most part remain silent on the behaviour of the citizens of Rome, for that of 1350 there is evidence that the less acceptable side of the religious life of the city was beginning to show. It is certain, for example, that there were a number of forged papal bulls circulating with the main purpose of making pilgrims stay longer in the city. One of these claimed that an indulgence could not be earned until a sequence of seven named churches had each been visited fifteen times. The vested interests in the daily trade provided by pilgrims for large sections of the Roman population were clearly very great.

Nevertheless, the popularity of the event was so enormous that even 50 years was thought then to be too long an interval. So in 1389, when the popes were again living in Rome, it was decided that as most people did not live for fifty years, the Jubilee should recur every thirty-three years - the number of years of Christ's life. In the following century even this was regarded as too infrequent, and in 1470 Pope Paul II, in order that every Christian should have a chance to visit Rome at least once in their lifetime during a Jubilee year, decreed that it should be celebrated every twenty-five years. So what in 1300 had begun as a spontaneous and unpremeditated form of celebration had, in less than two centuries, become an institution of worldwide fame, which must have transformed many aspects of Roman life. The overwhelming importance of Rome as a religious centre, coupled to the astonishing growth of indulgences, a system open to a limitless extension, was of course one of the causes of the revolt in northern Europe that brought about the Reformation.

It is perhaps hard for a modern mind to grasp the reality for the late medieval world-view of the spiritual gifts which the church lavished so liberally. Worldly gain would have been much less present as a motive than might be thought from the fourteenth century caricature of shameless greed immortalized by Chaucer in the 'Pardoner's Tale'. Here is an example of religious authority used for purely spiritual ends that was recorded as late as 1476. A bystander described how one day one of the great Renaissance popes, Sixtus IV, was visiting a convent of nuns - the 'Poor Clares' - in a town outside Rome. He was asked to grant them an indulgence, and did so, for the coming feast of the Birth of the Virgin. Then, perhaps, touched by the simplicity and virtue of their lives, he added that they could also have full immunity from guilt and penance on each occasion that they confessed their sins. This amazed the cardinals in the pope's entourage; they had never heard of any pope ever granting such an all-embracing indulgence, and asked Sixtus if he really meant that it should apply every single time. "Yes, indeed," he replied with his hand on his heart, "All that I have in my power to give, I give to them." At this the cardinals knelt before him and begged him to do the same for them. "Very well then," the Pope said, "I grant the same indulgence to you also." It is important to realize that Sixtus was a man of outstanding education and one of the great humanist popes of the Renaissance (it was he who built the Sistine Chapel); in spite of his great learning, he also had a complete and genuine faith in the medieval theological system that he had inherited. The eye-witness who reported this episode just saw an old man, moved by what he had seen of the transparent virtue of the Poor Clares, using his store of spiritual riches to give them, and then his cardinals, what he wished them to have.

We have seen how the religious life of Rome was to some extent lived on separate levels which would not normally have made much contact. Some events, however, would have united these different worlds, and undoubtedly the Jubilee would have had this effect. Other occasions on which a great event would have cut across the normal divisions would have been the coronation of a new pope, or the opening of a major church council. These celebrations would all have been marked by one of the most typical and spectacular of Roman manifestations - a public religious procession.

The city would have been accustomed to a sequence of annual processions, such as we have just seen occurred in January when the pope made his visitation to Sto. Spirito in Sassia. For each of the forty 'Stations' of Lent there would also have been a procession each day to the church where the pope was to say mass, and at other times of the year other churches would have been similarly honoured. More rarely, and therefore celebrated with more splendour, would have been the occasions when a church council was opened, a new building was inaugurated or when a new pope was crowned. For all of these occasions the pope would have travelled on a pre-ordained route that took in large tracts of the city, in order that he could be seen by the maximum number of people. The streets of the route to be taken would have been specially decorated, the houses decked with flowers and greenery and even, in some cases, lights and lanterns. At pre-arranged points the pope would stop to make presents of money to individual householders and, as we saw in the account of Adam of Usk, at other places he would throw handfuls of coins to the thronging crowds and so bring to a climax the hubbub and excitement of the occasion, as those present scrambled to pick them up.

These major processions would have united the different fields of the religious life of Rome to a greater extent than any other event, and a description of one of them written in the form of a letter to a friend, probably in Germany, has survived from the year 1215. The Fourth Lateran Council had just been inaugurated, being attended by bishops from all over the known world, including Constantinople and Jerusalem. The pope, Innocent III, took the opportunity to put on a great display of pomp for the reconsecration of a church which had been rebuilt in the previous century, that of Sta. Maria in Trastevere. He went in a spectacular procession from the Lateran, across Rome and over the Tiber into Trastevere. The anonymous medieval writer's description conveys well the day-long excitement of this spectacular event:

"The most noble of the Roman citizens, clad in purple cloaks and accompanied by singers and other musicians playing stringed and wind instruments, all making a great noise, were followed by an infinite crowd of people. Roman children bearing olive branches went out to meet them, saying after their custom 'Kyrie eleison, Christe eleison'. As soon as they had crossed over the bridge to the part of Rome where the church is [i.e. to Trastevere], they found the streets and squares lit by an innumerable quantity of lamps, hanging from ropes, which matched their warm glow to the mood of the occasion. It was not possible to count the flags of all colours that hung from the houses and high towers of the Romans. All the people attended the solemn dedication of the church, and heard the sermon; there is not space to tell you about the returning procession, but briefly I can say that the whole day was devoted to the consecration of the church, for it was not until vespers that the pope, with no less solemnity, went back through Rome to his palace."

(Author's translation)

We must let this fascinating account speak for itself - and for many other such colourful events which went unrecorded, but which united the population of Rome at the high moments of the celebration of their faith. There could be no more telling way of demonstrating the adulation by the Romans of a pope they loved, than to place him in the role of Christ entering Jerusalem, with children coming out of Trastevere to meet him, holding olive branches and singing.

V   The Arts in Medieval Rome

The buildings and art of any period or any culture must always, in some measure, reflect both the aspirations and the restrictions of their creators, and medieval Rome was certainly no exception to this. As the centuries passed and Roman life adjusted to successive regimes these aspirations would vary, as would the limitations imposed on them, but the history of Rome in the Middle Ages can be understood as readily in its architecture and its art as in any chronicle.

We have already seen how Constantine, the first Christian emperor, was responsible for the overall form of the city in a way that affected its development throughout the entire Middle Ages. The great building that he raised at the Lateran as the church of the bishop of Rome set both the scale and the type for innumerable later churches. The basilica, or 'royal hall', was the most common form of prestige building known to the Roman world, and examples could be found all over the empire; they would have varied only in their scale and in the richness of their decoration. This building also gave an 'official' character to the establishment of Christianity; none of the other religions that were practised in Rome at the beginning of the fourth century - Mithraism, Judaism, the worship of Isis - had buildings of such a scale or of such a prestigious character. So at the outset, although later remodelled many times, the Lateran basilica with its rich decoration and imperial origins gave the clearest possible expression to the Roman people of what their city was now to be.

Other buildings of this type followed in quite quick succession during the early fourth century: S. Croce in Gerusalemme, S. Sebastiano, S. Agnese, St. Peter's - this demonstrated both the aspirations of Rome and her leaders at that time, and the resources they had available. But the lavishness of these foundations was not to continue indefinitely; after St. Paolo in the late fourth century, and Sta. Sabina and Sta. Maria Maggiore in the fifth, Rome was not to see again buildings of this scale and grandeur until the Middle Ages closed. Whatever the great leaders of the later Middle Ages would have liked, they simply did not have the means to perpetuate the traditions of the early Christian centuries of Rome.

So if there is a pattern to be found in the tangled fabric that makes up the artistic life of the city as the medieval centuries passed, it is far more one of refurbishing and intermittent rebuilding of earlier structures than of a major succession of large-scale foundations continuing right through the Middle Ages. There is, for example, no building in Rome comparable with the astonishing outpouring of talent and skill represented by the sequence of great cathedrals in the Ile de France - Chartres, Amiens, Rheims and Nôtre Dame in Paris, to name only some. While these were rising above the level landscape of France, Rome saw virtually no new foundations, just a few substantial rebuildings of churches on the site of previous structures.

Another limitation to any discussion of the medieval art and architecture of Rome soon becomes apparent, and that is that the vast majority of surviving buildings are those with a religious function. Secular buildings of all kinds must have existed in large numbers, but their chances of survival were always smaller, and even those that have been allowed to remain standing to our own age have in every case been endlessly modernized by successive generations, often ending with a rather brutal restoration in this century.

The passion of the Romans for renovation and renewal of even their most venerated buildings is perhaps rather hard for our age to accept. Most countries of the developed world now have an extensive legislation specifically devised to preserve earlier buildings, or even entire areas of both urban or rural beauty. But this is a modern point of view which did not trouble most men of the Middle Ages, and certainly not the Roman people. It is indeed a symptom of their vitality that they could so readily dismantle or modernize their most hallowed buildings not just once, but over successive centuries.

The result of this robust and forthright approach is, of course, that we can see very few, if any, of the venerated buildings of Rome in anything like their original, or even their medieval, state. The natural disasters that the centuries bring have also taken their toll. Of the four great patriarchal basilicas of Rome, St. Peter's was finally demolished in the sixteenth century to make way for the building that we see today, S. Paolo was burnt down in 1823, and the Lateran basilica, where until the late nineteenth century the popes were still crowned, was remodelled completely in the seventeenth and eighteenth centuries, although not before it had been devastated by fires in 1308 and 1360. Only Sta. Maria Maggiore retains many of its principal features as they would have appeared in the later Middle Ages.

As monumental art forms such a vivid and complete mirror of Roman ideas and aspirations, we will consider a few buildings that, although only a tiny section of those still surviving in Rome, contain in their structure and decoration sufficient material to allow them to speak for the untold riches of the city's medieval past that have not come down to us.

Although untypical because of its great size, the basilica of Sta. Maria Maggiore does in other ways offer a brilliant microcosm of the huge range of art that was produced by the city in the millennium of its medieval existence. The original foundation was under Pope Liberius (352-366), and by tradition the site was held to have been revealed to a patrician Roman called John and to the pope by a miraculous fall of snow in August 352. For this reason the church was known by the titles of the Liberian basilica and that of Sta. Maria delle Neve (Our Lady of the Snow) before being given the dedication by which it is known today. This change of title can be quite a common Roman practice; it was also known for a time as Sta. Maria del Presepe in reference to the most revered of its relics - part of the crib of the infant Christ.

It was under Pope Sixtus III (342-440) that the basilica assumed its present size, and much of the original decoration still survives. It forms a fascinating commentary on the theological controversy that raged at the time which culminated in the resolutions of the church council held at Ephesus in 431. The brilliantly coloured mosaics covering the upper part of the triumphal arch leading into the chancel depict a number of scenes of New Testament subjects which emphasize the divinity of the Virgin as the

Mother of God, the *Theotokos*, who is shown here, for the first time, as an enthroned empress. There could be no clearer example of the use of imagery to give expression to a religious message, a feature of medieval art that was to reappear countless times. More mosaics from this original fifth-century scheme survive in the form of panels high above the columns all down the nave. These are of Old Testament subjects, and tend to concentrate on those episodes which concern ante-types of Christ from the Old Testament, such as Joshua, Moses and Abraham.

But the interest of these mosaics is not confined to their rarity or their subject-matter and location. Their style is a brilliant and prominent key to some of the solutions that artists of the period were forming when faced with the problems of establishing a new style in which to express the truths of their newly established religion. The pagan art of late antiquity had developed a robust naturalism which, because of its associations, could not be copied by Christian artists. Traces of the growing abstraction and de-materialization of this late antique style can be found in, for example, the art of the catacombs of the early Christians of Rome, but these mosaics in Sta. Maria Maggiore are the earliest major survivals which can be said to demonstrate the direction being taken by 'official' Christian art in the fifth century. The name of Sixtus III appears in the inscription on the triumphal arch mosaics, and he must have had personal knowledge of all their aspects. This gives them an authoritative position in the art of Rome in the early medieval period. The modern viewer of these mosaics will see that they are formed from tesserae (the name for the cubes, usually of coloured glass, which make up mosaic images) which do not follow the contours of the forms that are depicted, but are set in what we would now call an 'impressionistic' style. The figures often appear to be short and rather insubstantial, with their forms given a dematerialized quality by the reflecting facets of the hundreds of tesserae.

This 'early Christian style' of mosaic may well have been identified by later artists who wished to return to the ideals of the heroic period of early Christian Rome; the artist Giotto, who created a famous mosaic in St. Peter's many centuries later, seems to have adopted this style in a deliberate act of archaism, and so sought to remind his public of their great artistic traditions.

Sta. Maria Maggiore is typical of countless other churches in that it was the scene of a major work by the Cosmati workers. These were groups of craftsmen in marble who developed a particular style in the later Middle Ages that was largely identified with Rome and the surrounding region. It was probably in the mid-twelfth century that they completely re-laid the floor of Sta. Maria Maggiore in their own characteristic style of inlaid cut marble and mosaic. Although a radical restoration in 1750 prevent us from seeing it in its original state, the Cosmati workers have left here a memorial to their artistry and skill.

Yet again Sta. Maria Maggiore is typical of many other churches in that its apse mosaic was replaced at the end of the thirteenth century. We do not know what the subject of the original apse mosaic may have been, but it was probably a focus for the general theme of the establishment of the Virgin as the Mother of God as expressed in the mosaics of the arch. The hugely impressive image that rises above the visitor today as he approaches the apse is that of the Coronation of the Virgin by Christ, with attendant angels and saints. It is a subject that had only entered the repertory available to European artists relatively late, and then initially only in northern Europe, in the sculpture and glass of the great cathedrals. Below it the artist depicted in mosaic some scenes from the life of the Virgin, and that of her death was situated immediately beneath that of her Coronation in heaven. This arrangement again originated in France, and is an example of the influx of northern influence into the arts which we shall see took place around this time. This mosaic is also interesting from another point of view, in that it is one of the few works created before the fourteenth century of which we know the artist's name, in this case, Jacopo Torriti, and as such is symptomatic of a changing approach to artistic individuality in a wider context.

Also from around these years Sta. Maria Maggiore received another mosaic, installed this time on the west façade. Again, we know the name of the artist involved, Filippo Rusuti. Among the scenes in these mosaics is that concerning the legend of the foundation of the basilica under Pope Liberius, but they were

S. Paolo fuori le mura: facade mosaic by Cavallini of 1325-30. (18th century engraving by Piranesi). (Pl. 20)

S. Paolo fuori le mura: fresco paintings of Old Testament subjects on the North wall of the nave. (Engraved by Rossini just after the fire of 1823). (Pl. 21)

Sta. Maria Maggiore: facade mosaic of c. 1306-8 by Filippo Rusuti. 17th century drawing of the whole mosaic area. (Pl. 22)

The Forum with the Western exterior of the church of SS. Cosmas and Damian showing its romanesque campanile. (Pl. 23)

Sta. Maria Maggiore: facade mosaic - detail: the founding of the basilica by Pope Liberius in 352. (Pl. 24)

*Arch of Septimus Severus surmounted by a medieval tower; a drawing of
1504 by P.I. Breughel. (Pl. 25)*

*S. Giorgio in Velabro: fresco in the apse by Pietro Cavallini. Christ is flanked
by St. George, the Virgin, St. Peter and St. Sebastian. (Pl. 26)*

Sta. Maria in Trastevere: mosaic in the apse by Pietro Cavallini (late 13th century): votive mosaic with the donor. (Pl. 27)

Sta. Maria in Trastevere: mosaic of the nativity in apse.
(Pl. 28)

*Sta. Maria in Trastevere: detail of
the nativity mosaic: the piping
shepherd. (Pl. 29)*

*Sta. Maria in Aracoeli: tomb of Luca Savelli and family
(c. 1263). (Pl. 30)·*

St. Maria in Aracoeli: sarcophagus and effigy of Pope Honorius IV (1287).
(Pl. 31)

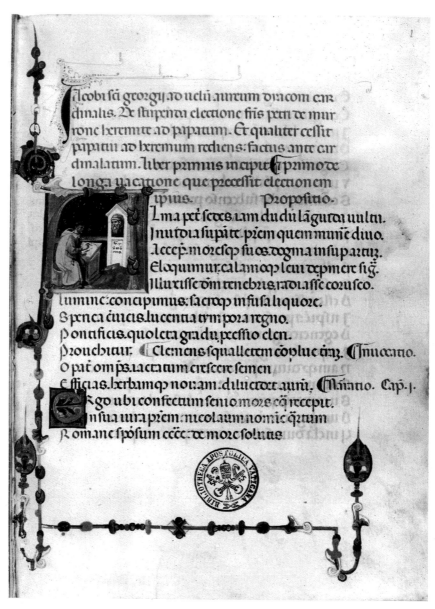

Manuscript of the 'Opus Metricum' of Jacapo Stefaneschi (early 14th century). (Pl. 32)

largely ruined in the eighteenth century when a baroque portico and balcony was constructed. However, there is still sufficient of the original scheme left for us to gain a clear idea of its colourful and imposing character.

So Sta. Maria Maggiore, with its legendary foundation, its early Christian mosaics, its renovations and restorations, the partial destruction of some its medieval features, can in many ways be seen as representative of what happened in innumerable other churches of Rome of more modest status.

The urge for constant renewal and revision of existing buildings, which forms such a prominent feature of the art and architecture of medieval Rome, had been given an early start when the large secular and public buildings of the city fell into disuse. We have seen how the pagan temples were steadily taken over, and other major buildings were being adapted during the early centuries of Christian life in the city. As the strength of the city's governmental life decreased, buildings connected with these functions became available for other uses. Just such a building was an imposing audience hall adjoining the Forum, which may have been the main office of the city prefect into the fourth and fifth centuries. Under Pope Felix IV (526-530) this came under ecclesiastical control and was converted into a church. The imposing mosaics on the arch and in the apse date from this time and show how the original dedication, to SS. Cosmas and Damian, has still been maintained, as these saints appear in the apse, with SS. Peter and Paul, and Felix IV, shown as a donor of the building. Their style shows that the mosaic tradition of fully-modelled forms and unambiguous physicality in the figures, the hallmark of antique figure style, had by no means died out. It is interesting to speculate on the date which might have been given to these mosaics had they survived without a named donor and with no documentary references; it would almost certainly have been much earlier.

A different fate befell another church in the Forum, nestling at the foot of the Palatine Hill. Originally a pagan building of the first century, it may have had some form of use as a guardroom for the important palace which it adjoined, until its use as a church in the sixth or seventh centuries. From then on, the church, known as Sta. Maria Antiqua until the mid-ninth century, had its walls covered with layer upon layer of frescoes, each new phase of decoration being painted on a fresh layer of plaster, so allowing the modern archaeologist to trace the successive styles of painting, one on top of the other. It is most unlikely that we would have been able to see these today had it not been for the fact that the building collapsed in a landslide in 847, to remain buried for almost a thousand years. Although it was rediscovered in the nineteenth century, it was only in 1900 that it was identified from document-ary records as the church known as Sta. Maria Antiqua.

Now, however, one can trace in these successive layers of decoration how different influences came and went in the art of Rome. The early eighth century, for example, was a period of considerable Greek influence in the city, with a Greek pope, John VII, on the throne of St. Peter, and many Greeks, both monks and laymen, fleeing to Italy to escape the persecutions of the icono-clasts in Constantinople. This is faithfully mirrored in the frescoes of Sta. Maria Antiqua, where a more fluid, Hellenistic style predominates at this time. This contrasts with an earlier, more hieratic and transcendental style that had emerged earlier, in the sixth and seventh centuries, and can still be seen in other monu-ments as well as in the rather sad ruin huddled at the foot of the Palatine.

Another church which demonstrates well the vicissitudes of Roman buildings over the centuries is that of S. Lorenzo-fuori-le-mura. Originally two separate buildings, of which the earliest was a fourth-century basilica, it was given its present form and propor-tions only in the early thirteenth century, when a cardinal, later to be Pope Honorius III, united a sixth-century church specially built by Pope Pelagius II with a newly built nave. The Pelagian church had been built into the hillside to allow pilgrims to visit the martyr's tomb, and it had mosaics on the arch into its chancel. These sixth-century figures now look down on the visitor from inside the present chancel, as the thirteenth-century remodelling involved the complete reversal of the Pelagian church, so that it became the chancel of the new and much enlarged basilica. Char-acteristically, this skilful piece of reconstruction had become necessary by reason of the steadily increasing flow of pilgrims during the Middle Ages; after the graves of St. Peter and St. Paul, that of St. Lawrence was one of the most revered in Rome, and his church on the via Labicana became one of the seven 'pilgrimage churches' of the city.

Typical also is the way the interior was refurnished from time to time, particularly over the period of the major rebuilding of Honorius III. From 1148 there can still be seen the richly inventive, if rather severe, canopy over the main altar. This must have already been in place before the thirteenth-century reconstruction, and is notable for being one of the early signed works of its kind. It is inscribed as being the work of the sons of the master-mason Paulus - Johannes, Petrus, Angelus and Sasso. The Cosmati workers were also active in S. Lorenzo; they gave the new basilica a superb marble and mosaic floor, an episcopal throne dated 1254, as well as a paschal candlestick. We get an interesting glimpse into the whole-hearted admiration in which the medieval Roman families held their classical past, as witnessed in the tomb in S. Lorenzo of Cardinal Fieschi. Here an antique Roman sarcophagus has been reused, with a mosaic and marble superstructure added to it. The cardinal, in common with other wealthy or aristocratic Romans of his age, particularly ecclesiastics, clearly found nothing incongruous in performing Christian burial rites over a sarcophagus carved with pagan reliefs.

S. Lorenzo was the only major Roman church to be damaged during the Second World War, when it was severely bombarded during an air raid in July 1943. This illustrates yet another hazard that time had in store for this major church, the fascination and beauty of which we can still enjoy today. The careful restoration took six years to complete.

A feature of a number of the most ancient of the Roman churches is how they were built in successive phases with one structure constructed literally on top of another. Often the earliest cult of a martyr would be focused on a small chapel or underground crypt; this was almost certainly the case with S. Lorenzo. As the cult of the martyrs grew, and the numbers of pilgrims increased, so new and larger buildings had to be built to house them. In a number of examples, the original burial places of the martyrs were outside the walls of Rome. Up until the eighth century the removal of the relics of these martyrs to a place of relative safety inside the city had not been approved; they should rest in peace, it was felt, where they had originally been buried. Pope Hadrian I was particularly active in this movement, which had a considerable effect on a number of Roman churches.

One church which illustrates better than any other the tendency to build one structure on top of another is that of S. Clemente. By the end of the fourth century a church had risen there, made from existing Roman buildings; these had in turn been erected on a yet earlier structure. In the ninth century the relics of St. Clement were removed there from outside the walls, and by 1099 it was of sufficient importance to be the site of the election of Pope Paschal II. But it was clearly felt to be inadequate for its current functions, as in 1128 a completely new basilica was dedicated and built immediately over the lower church. The new building had magnificent mosaics in the apse which can still be seen today, as well as a superb Cosmatesque pavement. Unlike most of the medieval churches of Rome, S. Clemente has kept the low, walled enclosure called the *schola cantorum*, in which the choir would stand for the services, as well as the two pulpits, or *ambones*, on either side. Although there are later additions in the form of tombs against the outside walls, and an eighteenth century painted ceiling, the interior of the upper church of S. Clemente still offers us one of the closest experiences to that of any worshipper in Rome. On a dark evening it takes little imagination to re-create the singing of vespers in the thirteenth century, with lamps and candles reflecting from the brilliant gold of the apse mosaics, and from the tesserae embedded in the marble interior furnishings of the Cosmati. To descend from this to the lower church is to take a step backward in time of some two centuries. The robust, almost harsh colours of the wall-paintings there, contrast with the more elegant and even sophisticated vine-scrolls drawn in the gold of the apse above. It is interesting that had it not been for the curiosity and energy of an Irish priest, Father Mulooly, who first excavated and discovered the lower church in 1857, this contrast might still be hidden from us today.

The most extensive of the many ensembles of medieval mosaics that can still be experienced is that of Sta. Prassede. The basilica, again built originally on Roman houses, was entirely rebuilt by Paschal I (817-824) who donated the superb mosaics on the arch, in the apse and, most impressive of all, on account of their completeness and small, enclosing scale - all over the interior of the chapel of S. Zeno. The pope, who can still be seen in the mosaic of the apse holding a model of the church, transferred many relics there from the catacombs, and the small chapel of S. Zeno must have been thought of as a precious container, almost like a jewelled casket, holding in safety these most revered remains of the early martyrs. Sta. Prassede was never to become one of the famous pilgrimage churches of the city, and so was never enlarged to any major extent. Paschal I even erected beside it a monastery for Greek monks, suggesting that the site and the dedication were not of any special significance for the Romans. A ninth-century visitor would have heard prayers being said in Greek in the oratory of S. Zeno, and Greek chants from the monks' choir.

The last two of these Roman churches which tell us, through their successive rebuildings and phases of redecoration, so much of the sequence of Roman artistic life are both in the area of Rome known as Trastevere, the area 'across the Tiber'. The first of them we have already met - it is the basilica of Sta. Maria in Trastevere, and is certainly the first Christian church in Rome to be dedicated to the Virgin, and may even be one of the earliest, officially recognized Christian buildings of the whole city. It was built near a hostel for veteran Roman soldiers, the legend runs, and on the day of Christ's birth in Palestine, a fountain of oil sprang up there, and flowed for a whole day down into the Tiber. To this day, the visitor approaches the piazza in front of the church through the 'Via del Fonte d'Olio'.

The foundation dates from the time of Pope Julius I (337-352), but it was on the site of an earlier building. The present scale of the basilica is entirely the result of a complete reconstruction under Innocent II (1130-1143). He was a member of the Papareschi family who lived in Trastevere, and it must have been a matter of family pride that he had the magnificent apse mosaic installed in which he is shown looking down on the faithful in the company of five saints and martyrs from the early centuries of the Roman church. The figures stand on either side of a new kind of image, that of the Virgin and Christ seated together on a double throne, and the texts that they hold are taken from the Song of Solomon, emphasizing the Virgin's role as the Queen of Heaven. He clearly intended to leave his mark on Trastevere, as he also must have initiated the superb mosaics on the triumphal arch inside the church, and may even have been responsible for starting the mosaic frieze on the outside façade of the church. It now appears to be the result of several different periods and styles, and has in many cases been restored so that there is now little agreement on the period of its inception, but, like the apse mosaic, its subject-matter seems without precedent. It shows the Virgin enthroned, suckling the infant Christ, and approached from either side by five richly clothed women, each of whom is carrying a lamp; in some cases the lamps have gone out, and these figures are shown without haloes. It is possible that the subject was intended to be that of the Wise and Foolish Virgins, and later restoration has made the subject more ambiguous than it was originally. The two small donor figures at the feet of the Virgin seem to be thirteenth century, and it may well be that the remaking of the façade mosaics has disguised their original appearance.

Another of the rich families of Trastevere, which rose to prominence during the thirteenth century and supplied at least one senator to the city's government on the Capitol, was the Stefaneschi. Their family seat was near to Sta. Maria in Trastevere, and at the end of the thirteenth century one of the sons of the family, Bertoldo, paid for a series of mosaic scenes to be installed in the apse of the church below those of the twelfth century. Like those in Sta. Maria Maggiore they concern the life of the Virgin, but have a more strongly developed narrative sense, and one can find in their sense of measured interval and graphic gesture, a premonition of the coming revolution in the arts with which Giotto's name is inextricably linked. Again, we know the name of their creator, Pietro Cavallini, and it is indeed possible that Giotto, who was the younger of the two, and who is known to have been in Rome over these years, learnt a great deal from him. Cavallini was to work in many other churches in the city, including both St. Peter's and S. Paolo, and must have been the best known of all the city's native artists. His life and work indeed signal a new phase in the public and social status of the artist as Cavallini was eventually buried in the basilica of S. Paolo, and over two centuries later a lamp was still being kept burning over his grave.

This was to be the last of the major medieval changes to the appearance of Sta. Maria in Trastevere. A rather drastic modernization took place in the nineteenth century which affected the character of the interior but left the medieval mosaics of the apse in their original state, and chapels and tombs were added during the intervening centuries. But to stand at the altar and look up at Cavallini's mosaics and those above of the twelfth century is still to gain an authentic experience of the medieval mosaicist's art as it changed and developed in the century and a half between the two phases of decoration.

Also in Trastevere is the church of Sta. Cecilia, and this again contains many successive layers of building and use. Above Roman houses, which had been used for church purposes by the third century, the present church was built by Pope Paschal I (817-824). He brought martyrs' relics from the catacombs, and marked his actions by having his own portrait installed in the superb mosaics in the apse. Although they have since been restored, they are still a brilliant example of the flatter and more linear style of mosaic, dependent on Byzantine rather than native early Christian traditions, that had been established by the ninth century. In the later eleventh century new altars were consecrated in the nave, and then Cavallini was again active here, this time painting in fresco the entire nave and west wall during the 1290s. Also from this time is the delicately carved ciborium over the high altar. It is by the sculptor, Arnolfo di Cambio, and shows unmistakably how French Gothic, decorative ideas were now beginning to take root in Rome. It is impossible to explain the beautiful ornamentation, the pointed trefoil arches and the crocketed pinnacles without assuming some experience on the sculptor's part of French taste and northern predilections. Yet the Cosmatesque areas of coloured inlay and the grasp of sculptural form shown in the carving of the figures, which could only have been learnt from the study of antique Roman sculpture, are sure signs of Arnolfo's Roman origins.

It was quite common to cover the interior of medieval churches with painted decoration, and although in most cases this has now disappeared, in Sta. Cecilia it is still possible for a modern visitor to gain some idea of what Cavallini's frescoes would have looked like. By one of those happy chances of history, when the titular cardinal of Sta. Cecilia restored the church in 1724, installing a new roof and building an enclosed choir gallery, some of the wall paintings were preserved. They were hidden behind choir-stalls in the nuns' choir (it was an enclosed order) and fragments can still be seen along the walls and above the later wooden roof. Although sadly damaged, those that have survived give us a clear idea of the character of the interior as it would have appeared in the early eighteenth century. Again, the sense of restrained interval that we saw in Cavallini's mosaics is also found here, and the fully modelled forms of his figures indicate the new attitude to the figure that was dawning in Italy.

The sequence of churches that has been briefly discussed here can all still be visited and, through the overlay of later taste that has in most cases drastically altered the overall impression, surviving features or fragments such as have just been described have to serve as a basis for re-creation of a unity that has passed. For the most part, interiors would have been considerably darker than they are today. There would have been little or no seating. The pews and benches which today occupy so much of the floor-space of these churches obscure the rich, geometric patterns that were clearly such a delight to the Cosmati workers as they laid out their colourful floor designs. While in some ways there was an immense respect for the past, with the hallowed memories of the early martyrs being given an ever greater prominence as the centuries unfolded, the Romans paid little attention to the actions of predecessors of only two or three centuries. Their pride in the city of the present was often stronger than their reverence for the achievements of their forbears. Even in the most prominent of the basilicas, tombs would be dismembered, paintings of earlier periods could be covered with different ones of a more modern style, and mosaics completely renewed. What in our age would be regarded as vandalism seems to have been commonplace where the art of earlier ages was concerned. For the Romans it seems that art was a powerful language which was only relevant if spoken in a modern accent. It was the physical remains and relics of the earliest days that were revered, such as the manger of the nativity in Sta. Maria Maggiore, the Veronica in St. Peter's, and these could not be renewed or replaced.

What the modern visitor cannot do is see the two most venerated of all the churches of Rome, St. Peter's and S. Paolo. If he had visited either of these in the years around the time of the papal migration to Avignon, he would have experienced an interior comparable in many ways to that of Sta. Maria Maggiore, only in both cases the broad naves were flanked by four aisles, not two. The destruction of these two supremely important and sacred buildings is a tragedy for anyone studying the art of medieval Rome. Because of their origins, they were the model for many comparable later buildings, as were the paintings to be found in them. Down the nave of S. Paolo, for example was a long sequence of scenes from Genesis and Exodus on one side, and a narrative cycle of scenes from the life of St. Paul on the other. Because of the early origins of these paintings, they went back to the origins of the church itself and were copied and adapted on innumerable occasions all over Europe. Carolingian Bible illustrations were probably based in part on the Old Testament cycle, as were ivory carvings in Southern Italy and mosaics in Sicily. The scenes from the life of St. Paul were equally influential; pilgrims to the saint's shrine would have studied each of these forty-odd compositions and discussed their content, so that when in Germany or France, or elsewhere in Italy or even in Greece artists were asked to celebrate some aspect of the saint's life the paintings in S. Paolo would, as often as not, be their source. The importance of these paintings to the Romans is indicated by the fact that at different times they were restored or repainted. The artist Cavallini, mentioned above, undertook just such a task in the late thirteenth century, just before working in Sta. Cecilia, and his frescoes in the nave there depicting Old Testament subjects in some measure reflected those in S. Paolo on which he had recently been working. St. Peter's, for some reason, was never endowed with such an influential series of monumental paintings, although its walls and its façade were covered in frescoes and mosaics from many different periods. While Pietro Cavallini was the artist most associated with S. Paolo, Giotto was to become identified with St. Peter's, with his extensive paintings in the chancel and the world-famous mosaic of the 'Navicella' on the exterior.

It is because the monumental art of Rome was so inescapably important to the medieval Romans, and therefore such a marvellous record for us today of their outlook, their thinking and their needs, that we have devoted the first part of this chapter to giving a view, albeit sketchy and impressionistic, of a little of it that remains. The visitor at the time of the Jubilee would have been able to see an infinitely greater range of such work of which only one or two per cent could be seen today. In spite of this huge loss, it is still possible to draw some general conclusions about the way that different styles came into favour and then gave way to a new approach which in turn was superseded by yet another. We see how the plastic modelling of forms that we associate with the art of antiquity had given way by the mid fifth-century to the more dematerialized, flatter figures of the Sta. Maria Maggiore mosaics. By the seventh century the figure had become a schematic, weightless image without any substance, but in the early eighth century, under Greek influence, this had given way to a more fully-rounded, Hellenistic approach. This was not to persist, however, and the ninth-century mosaics that survive indicate a return to the traditions of the sixth and seventh centuries. This austerity was gradually to disappear in the twelfth century, and with the thirteenth there is a clear renewal of the infinitely exciting possibilities of a richer exploitation of materials. While the concept of 'Renaissance' or 'Revival' is not a very appropriate one to apply to much of Roman art, the historical circumstances of the city certainly suggest that this was a century of great activity and experiment, culminating in the emergence of some of the first artistic personalities known to us from the whole Middle Ages. Yet even this brilliant period was to tail off rapidly when the popes left for Avignon, leaving a city largely bereft of its artists.

Yet while monumental painting and mosaic was perhaps the most characteristic form of Roman art, there were also many other forms of artistic expression. The Romans were, after all, heirs to the immensely powerful traditions of antique sculpture, and at all times this was a medium that would have been much in evidence; decorative carving on all kinds of buildings, tombs and effigies would all have been products of the sculptor's art. Yet here again, we find that there was a proud disregard for the work of earlier generations; when Arnolfo di Cambio carved the canopies over the high altars of S. Paolo and Sta. Cecilia, he seems to have re-used sculpture from the ninth or tenth centuries. This became clear when, as a result of the fire of 1823 that destroyed most of S. Paolo, the canopy had to be rebuilt and the earlier carving was found when the construction was dismantled.

There was also demand for secular sculpture, although this does not seem to have been very consistent. Well-heads survive from the ninth and tenth centuries, and door-jambs and lintels from later periods. The build-up of artistic production towards the end of the thirteenth century included sculpture created for largely political ends. To emphasize his position as the protector of Rome, Charles of Anjou had a life-size portrait sculpture of himself carved by Arnolfo di Cambio, and it was set up in Sta. Maria in Aracoeli, just next to the Capitol. In the next few years this example was followed by some of the popes; although for religious leaders, the function of these 'cult images' was almost purely political. Initially, perhaps for this reason, these statues were only erected outside Rome, with the clear intention of extending the pope's influence to where his person was seldom, if ever, seen. Nicholas III and Nicholas IV both used sculpture in this way, and each under the guise of commemorating a legal decision in which the pope had found in favour of the city where the sculpture was to be set up. But Boniface VIII brought the tradition into Rome itself, with an image of himself set up at the Lateran, as well as with others as far afield as Orvieto, Florence and even Amiens. It is probably from this time, too, that the bronze statue of the en-throned St. Peter comes, which can still be seen in St. Peter's and from which the metal of the foot is worn smooth by the lips of countless millions of pilgrims down the centuries. But sculpture, perhaps surprisingly, does not seem to have played such an important part in the art of medieval Rome as mosaic and fresco. It may have been the association with the pagan past that proved stronger than the expressive possibilities of the medium.

But although the monumental arts of mosaic, fresco-painting and sculpture could certainly be said to provide the dominant strands in the artistic life of medieval Rome, the visual arts also took many other forms. Easel-painting was certainly practised, and we also know that workshops existed for the illumination of manuscripts. All portable paintings would have been on panel, of course (canvas was an innovation of the Renaissance), and the losses would have been colossal. Judging from the known panel paintings that have survived, we may now only have one or two per cent of those that were in existence during the twelfth and thirteenth centuries. But every one of the hundreds of churches that are known to have been in use would have had some form of altar-piece depicting the dedicatee, and some may well have had a number, sited over side altars. In some cases these paintings would have taken the form of 'cult images', some even credited with miraculous powers. Towards the end of the medieval period the form and lay-out of these altar-pieces began to change, and narrative scenes and other episodes began to be included. This transitional period can be seen in, for example, a painting that Giotto created to be placed on the high altar of St. Peter's, and which is now in the Vatican. In it we can see not just an enthroned image of Christ surrounded by angels, with an image of the cardinal who commissioned the work, but scenes of the martyrdoms of St. Peter and St. Paul. But for most of the later Middle Ages these paintings on panel would have been usually of one or two figures placed in hieratic isolation, and with their eyes fixed on the beholder in a remote and timeless gaze. Just such a panel was found in the church of Sta. Maria in Trastevere, which has already been mentioned. Here the regal figure of the enthroned Virgin, with Christ on her knee and supported on either side by an angel, looked out on its devotees for over twelve centuries, as it is dated by an inscription to the early eighth century.

In the case of manuscript illumination, it is perhaps surprising that there has apparently not been a more continuous tradition in Rome. While there must always have been several centres of manuscript production, or scriptoria, in the city, most of what these produced need have had no illustrations. They would have been records, copies of letters and other documents, agreements of a legal nature, wills, and material of many other kinds that did not need any illustration or illumination. It would have been almost exclusively, in the case of liturgical and religious works, that manuscripts would have been passed on to artists after the scribes had completed their work on the text. A scriptorium of this kind, which employed artists as well as scribes, was certainly active in the monastery attached to Sta. Cecilia in Trastevere from the late eleventh century and throughout most of the twelfth. Besides Gospel books with illustrations of the evangelists, which was a fairly common kind of product, this scriptorium also participated in the making of a typically Roman kind of book. This was a version of the Bible on a huge scale. They are now known as Giant Bibles, and one that was produced in Sta. Cecilia around the turn of the eleventh and twelfth centuries is still today in the Vatican Library. It has illustrations to a number of passages, and many decorated initial letters. The character of the artistry is not very sophisticated, but its directness and vigour, combined with the scale of the whole work, speaks eloquently of this period of Roman medieval art.

There must in the nature of normal probability have been at least one scriptorium producing illuminated manuscripts during the great artistic expansion of the later thirteenth century, but if there was, its products are hard to establish. Unlike monumental art, manuscripts travel far and wide and, with no signatures or artists' names on them, it becomes very hard to know for certain if a possible Roman origin is any more than just a possibility. There were other much better-established centres of illumination, such as Bologna, and it is possible that manuscripts written in Rome could, if sufficiently important and worth the expense, have been sent there for the addition of their miniatures, or that a Bolognese illuminator could work for a time in Rome. Just such a 'problem' work is the immensely sumptuous Bible now in the British Museum that was for a long time in the library of Holkham Hall, hence its name, the Holkham Bible.

But for the medieval world, painting and sculpture were just part of the whole field of artistic production; the distinction between the 'fine arts' and the 'applied arts' did not exist. In any major city there would also have been much to see of work in metal and in textile products, and Rome was certainly no exception here. Besides the papal processions, and other ecclesiastical functions, there would also have been many secular events when senators and the representatives of the *Rioni* clearly enjoyed showing off their splendour. Not only do we know of individual events of this kind, which were specifically recorded, as when Cola di Rienzo had himself clothed in white silk embroidered in gold, and equipped with a golden belt and spurs, but there were also many regular occasions for spectacular processions and ceremonial. For instance, at the time of the Carnival, each of the thirteen *Rioni* would provide a bull which was taken in procession, garlanded with spring flowers and accompanied by richly dressed citizens, from the Piazza Agone (now called Piazza Navona) to the Capitol. All civic events concerning the senate which were the focus of Roman popular pride, would have put on a luxurious display of colourful wealth. Besides regalia in precious metal (each senator, for example, needed to have three rings, one with a ruby, one with a diamond and one with an emerald), the quantities of richly colourful fabrics would have been spectacular.

The loss of all these luxury art products from the Middle Ages has been vast; only small numbers of works in metal have survived, and even fewer in the more fragile form of textiles. Yet when attempting to reassemble in the mind's eye one of these medieval Roman public events, the loss, relative to the effect that it would have created at the time, has probably been greatest in the field of brocades, silks and velvets. Our knowledge of what existed in Rome comes from written sources such as wills and inventories. That made at the end of the thirteenth century of the papal treasury under Boniface VIII lists vast quantities of goods that have now mostly vanished, but rich vestments were certainly much in evidence, with dalmatics, chasubles and copes listed among the thirteen mitres and other textile items.

It is tempting to visualize a unity of taste that might have existed between the patterned silks and brocades, the sumptuous objects of precious metal, and the monumental art of the painters and mosaicists, the sculptors and the inlaid and encrusted marble of the Cosmati workers. This unity could be taken to be a specifically 'Roman' taste of the medieval period. Yet it is unlikely that such a comprehensive style existed, for the reason that much of these 'luxury arts' were imported.

To build up a tradition of skilled work in precious metals needs long-term stability, combined with quite a high level of prosperity. Craftsmen need not just well-equipped workshops and a supply of skilful assistants, but also access to supplies of bullion. The fact is that Rome, although it knew periods of prosperity, and for much of the Middle Ages could have provided rich patronage of all kinds, does not seem to have furnished the right kinds of conditions for the establishment of a tradition of goldsmithing. Siena and Florence, with Venice and perhaps Naples, were the main centres in later medieval Italy for this trade, as Pisa, Lucca, Palermo and Venice were renowned for the manufacture and trading in rich textiles. In Boniface VIII's treasure, there were items of both apparel and metalware that came from as far afield as England. Yet we know that in the later thirteenth century the popes had more than once been forced to raise loans from Roman banks, and pledged the church's property as security. In the more steadily prosperous city of Siena this would never have occurred.

So while Romans would have seen quantities of richly colourful clothing and jewels in public processions of all kinds, it is unlikely that much of it was actually made in the city. The teams of mosaicists, fresco-painters, sculptors and Cosmati workers would have fully demonstrated the 'Roman' medieval artistic tradition, while works in metal would, by contrast, have been representative of a more northern style. What has survived has decoration that owes a lot to that found on Gothic architecture, a style foreign to Italy, but at home in central France. Textiles, in turn, would have reflected eastern or north Italian taste, as most of the richer examples came from areas under these influences.

Before leaving the subject of the arts in medieval Rome, it is interesting to assess the conditions of patronage under which it was produced. This is a complex field about which all too little is known, but in order to understand the way that the arts developed in the city, it is important to consider this aspect. It involves not just the artists and craftsmen who produced the works, but also those who were employing them, and the whole field is intimately linked to other studies - social and political history, changing economic conditions, and the rise and fall of fashions and artistic styles in countries outside Italy altogether.

Patronage of the arts in Rome must always have presented a more complex picture than in most other European cities. Its position as the centre of the Catholic Church would have at once made it a focus of monumental art of a specifically public purpose, that of impressing all who lived in or visited the city with the ever-present aura of its unique claims. Only one other city in the world could at times have matched the splendour and quantity of the public display of art that could be found in the churches of Rome, and that was Constantinople, the 'New Rome' founded on the Bosphorus which was to become the centre of the other principal Christian hierarchy. But given the fact that the arts played a more public part in Rome than might have been the case in other cities, it is interesting to speculate who were the individuals who initiated these schemes and provided the general conditions under which artists could work to such brilliant effect. For much of the city's medieval existence the chief wealth that would have been available for expenditure on the arts would have been in the hands of either the powerful feudal families of Rome and the surrounding country, or those of the pope and, to a lesser extent, his immediate entourage. At times, as we have seen, these two forces would coincide. In the ninth century, for example, the reigns of Leo III and Paschal I were marked by much activity in building and the arts, and both these popes were of Roman stock. The balances of influence and wealth were always changing, but the tendency during the later Middle Ages was for the church revenues to be spread more broadly over the individuals in the curia. This was a reflection of the increasing importance of the cardinals in church government, and this was actually confirmed by a papal decree of 1289 which allotted half of the papal revenues to the cardinals. As the popes were much of the time obliged to spend their revenues on political and military projects, the cardinals, particularly if they were already of rich families, could be in a position to spend more on artistic enterprises than the popes themselves. Certainly a number of the cardinals, towards the end of the thirteenth century, lived in large palaces with extensive households, and impressed visitors to the city with the splendour of their lifestyle.

For the arts of Rome, this situation tended to make for a greater variety of taste being expressed, as this 'ecclesiastical aristocracy' could contain members of various nationalities and outlook. Even in St. Peter's in the years around 1300, the pilgrims would have seen wall-paintings in the chancel, the main altar-piece on the high altar (the focus of devotion for the whole western church) and the mosaic of the Navicella in the atrium, all paid for by one of the wealthiest of the cardinals, Jacopo Stefaneschi. Not long before Nicholas III had had a series of papal portraits created in mosaic down each side of the nave, and Cavallini had been employed to paint some giant figures of the evangelists. The fact is that the most prominent and impressive works of art in the most important church in Europe were only the result of one cardinal's patronage, rather than that of a pope. At the same time, in S. Paolo, Arnolfo di Cambio constructed the magnificent ciborium over the high altar, which clearly displays an admiration for the gothic style which had been spreading from its home ground in the Ile de France to different parts of Europe.

Gothic was never completely at home under the Roman sun; it was a style that must have been imported by French, or Francophile, clerics, and so forms part of the complex pattern of foreign patronage in the city. It appears in other altar canopies, in tombs, and most prominently of all in the only church in Rome built in the gothic style: Sta. Maria sopra Minerva. But one always feels that the severe columns and stone beams of the Cosmati ciboria, and the open spacious hall of the nave of Sta. Maria in Aracoeli, are a more authentic expression of the Roman artistic spirit than the pointed arches and tracery of a style that was at home north of the Alps.

So as the visitor left Rome, and paused to look back on the 'cornfield of towers' that was the most striking aspect of the medieval city seen from afar, what would have been the most striking impressions of the art that he had seen? The mosaics and wall-paintings of the major churches would have provided his most powerful memories. No other city that he could see in western Europe could have demonstrated such a wealth of this art, which would always be identified as an essentially Roman art. By the later thirteenth century the contribution of the Cosmati would have been prominent, and their brilliant and colourful patterns, set off by the white marble in which their mosaics were set, would also have been a most powerful image and, again, unique to Rome and the surrounding area. And thus it was that the arts that were most intimately connected with building came to be seen as synonymous with Roman art, and it was the memory of these which would have remained most vividly with the visitor as he journeyed home. Art on a smaller scale, such as manuscripts, paintings on panel, objects in precious metal, would probably have made less impression as they were seen only in passing, or at a distance. The art of Rome in the Middle Ages was, above all, an art that projected a Christian message to a vast and changing audience; its impact had to be substantial and enduring. It would always be the art of the Eternal City.

Appendix

A chronological list of the popes of Rome from the age of Constantine to the return from Avignon. Antipopes have not been included.

Marcellus I	308-309	Pelagius II	579-590	Hadrian I	772-795
Eusebius	309-310	Gregory I	590-604	Leo III	795-816
Miltiades	311-314	Sabianus	604-606	Stephen V	816-817
Sylvester	314-335	Boniface III	607	Paschal I	817-824
Mark	336	Boniface IV	608-615	Eugenius II	824-827
Julius I	337-352	Deodatus I	615-618	Valentine	827
Liberius	352-366	Boniface V	619-625	Gregory IV	827-844
Damasus	366-384	Honorius I	625-638	Sergius II	844-847
Siricius	384-399	Severinus	640	Leo IV	847-855
Anastasius I	399-401	John IV	640-642	Benedict III	855-858
Innocent I	401-417	Theodore I	642-649	Nicholas I	858-867
Zosimus	417-418	Martin I	649-655	Hadrian II	867-872
Boniface I	418-422	Eugenius I	655-657	John VIII	872-882
Celestine I	422-432	Vitalian	657-672	Marinus I	882-884
Sixtus III	432-440	Deodatus II	672-676	Hadrian III	884-885
Leo I	440-461	Donus	676-678	Stephen VI	885-891
Hilary	461-468	Agatho	678-681	Formosus	891-896
Simplicius	468-483	Leo II	682-683	Boniface VI	896
Felix III	483-492	Benedict II	684-685	Stephen VII	896-897
Gelasius I	492-496	John V	685-686	Romanus	897
Anastasius II	496-498	Conon	686-687	Theodore II	897
Symmachus	498-514	Sergius I	687-701	John IX	898-900
Hormisdas	514-523	John VI	701-705	Benedict IV	900-903
John I	523-526	John VI	705-707	Leo V	903
Felix IV	526-530	Sisinnius	708	Sergius III	904-911
Boniface II	530-532	Constantine	708-715	Anastasius III	911-913
John II	533-535	Gregory II	715-731	Landonius	913-914
Agapetus I	535-536	Gregory III	731-741	John X	914-928
Silverius	536-537	Zacharias	741-752	Leo VI	928
Vigilius	538-555	Stephen II	752	Stephen VIII	928-931
Pelagius I	556-561	Stephen III	752-757	John XI	931-935
John III	561-574	Paul I	757-767	Leo VII	936-939
Benedict I	575-579	Stephen IV	768-772	Stephen IX	939-942

Marinus II	942-946	Leo IX	1049-1054	Gregory IX	1227-1241
Agapetus II	946-955	Victor II	1055-1057	Celestin IV	1241
John XII	955-964	Stephen X	1057-1058	Innocent IV	1243-1254
Leo VIII	963-965	Nicholas II	1059-1061	Alexander IV	1254-1261
Benedict V	964	Alexander II	1061-1073	Urban IV	1261-1264
John XIII	965-972	Gregory VII	1073-1085	Clement IV	1265-1268
Benedict VI	973-974	Victor III	1086-1087	Gregory X	1271-1276
Boniface VII	974	Urban II	1088-1099	Innocent V	1276
Benedict VII	974-983	Paschal II	1099-1118	Hadrian V	1276
John XIV	983-984	Gelasius II	1118-1119	John XXI	1276-1277
Boniface VII	984-985	Callixtus II	1119-1124	Nicholas III	1277-1280
John XV	985-996	Honorius II	1124-1130	Martin IV	1281-1285
Gregory V	996-999	Innocent II	1130-1143	Honorius IV	1285-1287
Sylvester II	999-1003	Celestin II	1143-1144	Nicholas IV	1288-1292
John XVII	1003	Lucius II	1144-1145	Celestin V	1294
John XVI	1004-1009	Eugenius III	1145-1153	Boniface VIII	1294-1303
Sergius IV	1009-1012	Anastasius IV	1153-1154	Benedict XI	1303-1304
Benedict VIII	1012-1024	Hadrian IV	1154-1159	Clement V	1305-1314
John XIX	1024-1032	Alexander III	1159-1181	John XXII	1316-1334
Benedict IX	1032-1044	Lucius III	1181-1185	Benedict XII	1334-1342
Sylvester III	1044-1045	Urban III	1185-1187	Clement VI	1342-1352
Benedict IX	1045	Gregory VIII	1187	Innocent VI	1352-1362
Gregory VI	1045-1046	Clement III	1187-1191	Urban V	1362-1370
Clement II	1046-1047	Celestin III	1191-1198	Gregory XI	1370-1378
Benedict IX	1047-1048	Innocent III	1198-1216		
Damasus II	1048	Honorius III	1216-1227		

Notes on Illustrations

Pl.1   Sta Costanza: section of vault mosaic with portrait head. This is thought to be a portrait of Constantina (d. 354); the vine-scrolls which surround it allude to the theme of the day of judgement, suggesting that the building was intended to serve as her mausoleum. *(Ist. Centrale per il Catalogo e la Documentazione, Roma, ser. C, neg. 2207.)*

Pl.2   Sta Maria Maggiore: detail of mosaic on the triumphal arch. These mosaics were installed by Pope Sixtus III (432-440), and their style displays the de-materialization that was developed by early Christian artists in contrast to the more naturalistic forms of classical art. *(Alinari.)*

Pl.3   Sta Prassede: vault mosaic in Chapel of S. Zeno. This small, jewel-like chapel was built by Pope Paschal I (817-824) as a mausoleum for his mother, and is the only such building in Rome to have its interior entirely covered in mosaic. *(The Conway Library, Courtauld Institute of Art.)*

Pls.4-5 Church of the Quattro Coronati; frescoes in the Capella di S. Silvestro. These 12th century frescoes, in the pronounced linear style of medieval Roman painting, depict the legend of Constantine, the first Christian emperor. He had been smitten with leprosy, and had been told by pagan priests that if he bathed in the blood of three thousand Roman children he would be cured. When he arrived at Rome he was, according to the legend, so moved by the grief of the children's mothers that he refused to have them slaughtered, and later, when he was baptised by Pope Sylvester, he was cured of his leprosy.

    - the women of Rome lamenting before Constantine *(Pl.4)*
    - the baptism of Constantine by Pope Sylvester. *(Alinari)* *(Pl.5)*

Pl.6 Anagni, the Duomo: the large fresco cycle in the crypt here, dating from the mid-13th century, contains this battle scene in one of its vaults. Anagni, a short distance form Rome, was the seat of the Gaetani family, and was to be the scene of the outrage committed on Pope Boniface VIII. *(Ist. Centrale per il Catalogo e la documentazione, Roma, ser. E, neg. no. 48693.)*

Pl.7 St Peter's: this 17th century water-colour of the nave wall and its severely damaged paintings gives some of the most detailed evidence for the appearance of the interior during the Middle Ages. *(Archivio S. Pietro, Album, fol.13. Foto Biblioteca Vaticana.)*

Pl.8 St Peter's: a 17th century water-colour showing the appearance of the entrance wall with altars and frescoes from various periods. *(Archivio S. Pietro, Album, fol.18. Foto Biblioteca Vaticana.)*

Pl.9 St John Lateran: this apse mosaic of 1290, showing Pope Nicholas IV (1288-1292) as a donor, was originally created by the artist Jacopo Torriti, but was renewed in the mid-19th century. *(Alinari)*

Pls.10-11 Sta Maria in Trastevere: this 12th century mosaic on the façade of the church is unique in Rome; the subject is thought to be based on the parable of the Wise and Foolish Virgins.

- detail: the Madonna and child in the centre *(Pl.10)*
- detail: wise virgins. *(Alinari) (Pl.11)*

Pls.12-14 Sta Maria Maggiore: the apse mosaic of c.1295 is the work of Jacopo Torriti, and is one of the earliest in Rome to bear the name of its artist.

- the whole apse. *(Alinari) (Pl.12)*
- detail: angels and the kneeling figure of Pope Nicholas IV, who died in 1292. *(Alinari) (Pl.13)*
- detail: the Dormition of the Virgin. *(Alinari) (Pl.14)*

Pl.15 Grenoble, Museum: a late 13th century Roman panel painting of St Lucy, with a female donor; her name is given as 'Angila, wife of Odo of the Cerroni family'. As St Lucy was invoked to cure maladies of the eyes, it is possible that the painting was commissioned as a votive offering to the saint for curing this member of an ancient Roman family. *(Photo Ifot.)*

Pl.16 From the '*Speculum Romanae Magnificentiae*' by Antonio Lafreri; this engraved aerial view of Rome was made in the later 16th century, but still clearly shows the form of the medieval city, with the densely packed houses of the *abitato* contrasting with the empty eastern sectors (the top of the plan is south). *(The Conway Library, Courtauld Institute of Art).*

Pl.17 Sta Maria in Aracoeli: tomb of Cardinal Matteo d'Acquasparta, with fresco by Pietro Cavallini (c.1302). This cardinal, who died in that year, was a Franciscan and was mentioned by Dante (*Paradiso XII*); he had been created cardinal by Boniface VIII in 1297. *(Alinari)*

Pl.18 Sta Cecilia in Trastevere: ciborium over the high altar by Arnolfo di Cambio, dated 1293. It is in works such as this that the Romans would have first experienced the forms of Gothic architecture that had developed north of the Alps. *(Ist. Centrale per il Catalogo e la documentazione, Roma, ser. E, neg. no. 9076.)*

Pl.19 Sta Cecilia in Trastevere: detail of fresco of the Last Judgement by Pietro Cavallini (late 13th century). The artist was one of the most influential figures in Roman art towards the end of the Middle Ages. These frescoes have only survived because they were covered by wooden choir-stalls when the church became the home of an enclosed order of nuns. *(Ist. Centrale per il Catalogo e la Documentazione, Roma, ser. C, neg. no. 11475.)*

Pl.20 S. Paolo fuori le mura: façade mosaic by Cavallini of 1325-30; (18th century engraving by Piranesi). The donor of this mosaic, Pope John XXII, was depicted in it, although at the time living in Avignon, and he must have intended that it should demonstrate his continuing authority in the city and his interest in its churches. The mosaic was destroyed after the fire of 1823.

Pl.21 S. Paolo fuori le mura: fresco paintings of Old Testament subjects on the north wall of the nave; (engraved by Rossini just after the fire of 1823). These frescoes viewed by countless thousands of pilgrims over the centuries, had been renewed in the later 13th century by Pietro Cavallini; the artist was later buried in the basilica, and a lamp was kept burning at his grave.

Pl.22   Sta Maria Maggiore: façade mosaic of c.1306-8 by Filippo Rusuti. This was one of several large projects of which members of the rich Colonna family were the patrons, and their armorial device can be seen in these mosaics. The mosaic was disfigured in the 18th century by the addition of a loggia.

- a 17th century drawing of the whole mosaic area. *(National Gallery of Scotland.)*

Pl.23   The Forum, with the western exterior of the church of SS. Cosmas and Damian (originally a 6th century foundation) showing its romanesque campanile, contrasting with the later medieval Tor de' Conti. (A 17th century drawing by Gillis van Valckenborch.)

Pl.24   Sta Maria Maggiore: façade mosaic of c.1306-8 by Filippo Rusuti.

- detail of the mosaic: the founding of the basilica by Pope Liberius in 352. *(Alinari)*

Pl.25   Arch of Septimus Severus surmounted by a medieval tower: a drawing of 1504 by P.I. Breughel. Many ancient Roman monuments were taken over and built on in this way. *(Devonshire Collection, Chatsworth. Reproduced by permission of the Chatsworth Settlement Trustees.)*

Pl.26   S. Giorgio in Velabro: fresco in the apse by Pietro Cavallini (c.1300-8). This is now damaged, but is still an impressive scheme, depicting Christ flanked by St George, the Virgin, St Peter and St Sebastian.

Pls.27-29   Sta Maria in Trastevere: mosaics in the apse by Pietro Cavallini (late 13th century). These mosaic scenes portraying events from the life of the Virgin were commissioned by a

112

member of the rich family of the Stefaneschi, who lived nearby in Trastevere.

- Votive mosaic with the donor, Bertoldo Stefaneschi. *(Alinari)* *(Pl.27)*
- Mosaic of the Nativity. *(Alinari)* *(Pl.28)*
- Detail of the Nativity mosaic: the piping shepherd. *(Lazio)* *(Pl.29)*

Pl.30   Sta Maria in Aracoeli: tomb of Luca Savelli and family, c.1263. The tomb may have been designed by the sculptor Arnolfo di Cambio, and the vivid inlaid mosaic is the work of the Cosmati, but its most prominent feature is the 3rd century antique Roman sarcophagus. *(The Conway Library, Courtauld Institute of Art.)*

Pl.31   Sta Maria in Aracoeli: Sarcophagus and effigy of Pope Honorius IV (Iacopo Savelli), d. 1287; the pope's tomb is in St Peter's. This decorative mosaic work on the sarcophagus is by the Cosmati family, and is a specifically Roman feature. *(The Conway Library, Courtauld Institute of Art.)*

Pl.32   Manuscript of the *Opus Metricum* of Jacopo Stefaneschi, Vat. lat. 4932, fol. 1r: early 14th century. This miniature illustrating Cardinal Stefaneschi's historical poem shows Pietro da Morrone, the saintly hermit on Mount Solmona, who had just been elected pope as Celestin V. *(Foto Biblioteca Vaticana.)*

Some Books for Further Reading

F. Gregorovius: *History of the City of Rome in the Middle Ages.* (Transl. by Mrs G.W Hamilton from the 4th German Edn.) 8 vols., London (Bell) 1909.

F. Gregorovius: *Rome and Medieval Culture. Selections from History of the city of Rome in the Middle Ages.* Edited and Introduced by K.F. Morrison. Chicago/London 1971.

G. Barraclough: *The Medieval papacy.* London (Thames & Hudson) 1958, repr. 1979.

R. Brentano: *Rome Before Avignon. A Social History of Thirteenth-Century Rome.* New York (Basic Books) 1974.

R. Krautheimer: *Rome, Profile of a City 312-1308.* Princeton 1980.

D. Waley: *The Papal State in the Thirteenth Century.* London 1969.

W. Oakeshott: *The Mosaics of Rome from the third to the fourteenth centuries.* London (Thames & Hudson) 1967.

E. Hutton: *The Cosmati. The Roman Marble Workers of the XIIth and XIIIth Centuries.* London (Routledge Kegan Paul) 1950.

Index